HOW LEVESQUE WON

The story of the PQ's
stunning
election victory

Pierre Dupont

D0220072

Translated by
Sheila Fischman

3 9345 01078771 5

NOUS·SOMMES·PRETS

SIMON FRASER UNIVERSITY
W.A.C. BENNETT LIBRARY

JL 258 D8513 c.2

HOW LEVESQUE WON

HOW LEVESQUE WON

Pierre Dupont

Translated by
Sheila Fischman

James Lorimer & Company, Publishers
Toronto   1977

Originally published as *15 Novembre 76*.
Copyright © 1976 by Les Editions Quinze.
Translation copyright © 1977 by James Lorimer & Company.
All rights reserved. No part of this book may be reproduced or transmitted in any form or by any means, electronic or mechanical, including photocopying, or by any information storage and retrieval system, without permission in writing from the publisher.

"For an Independent Quebec" copyright © 1976 by René Lévesque. Used by permission.

ISBN 0-88862-130-2 paper
ISBN 0-88862-131-0 cloth

Cover design: Don Fernley
Cover photo: GAMMA
Photographs: Canada-Wide

Printed and bound in Canada

5 4 3 2 1 77 78 79 80 81

James Lorimer & Company, Publishers
Egerton Ryerson Memorial Building
35 Britain Street
Toronto

Canadian Cataloguing in Publication Data

Dupont Pierre, 1947-
    How Levesque won

Translation of 15 Novembre 76.
ISBN 0-88862-131-0 bd. ISBN 0-88862-130-2 pa.

1. Quebec (Province) National Assembly - Elections, 1976. 2. Elections - Quebec (Province). 3. Parti québécois. 4. Quebec (Province) - Politics and government - 1960-   I. Title.

JL258.D8613   329'.023'71404   C77-001133-0

Contents

Translator's Note

I am grateful to Richard Cléroux of the *Globe and Mail,* Brian McKenna of CBC-TV's "The Fifth Estate," Stuart McLean of CBC-Radio's "Morningside" and Patrick Brown of the *Last Post* for research and moral support, and particularly grateful to Robert Chodos, a splendid, tactful editor.

S.F.

Introduction

On the morning of November 16, 1976, in the delegates' lounge at the United Nations, the diplomatic gossip was lively. The topic of the day: the accession to power of the Parti Québécois. Some people were already speculating about the seat for a prospective representative from Quebec — it would be immediately next to the one for Qatar. Others were hoping they would run into the Canadian delegate that day to find out how Ottawa was reacting.

For ten years now, when Canada has been talked about around the world it's been because of Quebec. Expo 67 captured the imagination of thousands of tourists and foreign dignitaries, and, for the first time, Montreal and Quebec became briefly the centre of world attention. Also in 1967, General de Gaulle's shout of "Vive le Québec libre!" resounded around the world and, for the world press, Quebec was born. Three years later FLQ terrorists carried off a double kidnapping: James Richard Cross, the British Trade Commissioner in Montreal, and Pierre Laporte, the Minister of Labour. These events too made the front pages of foreign newspapers; world reaction to the Canadian government's hard line was one of dismay. The immaculate image of the Canadian "peaceable kingdom" was considerably tarnished.

The next event to capture world attention was the imprisonment in 1972 of Quebec's three top union leaders. This was particularly surprising because such an action is rare in so-called democratic countries. Even in France, in May '68, it didn't happen. And news in the foreign press about preparations for the 1976 Olympic Games in Montreal was pessimistic and often even sarcastic. Much attention was paid to the presence of the Mafia, to violence in the construction industry, to waste and Mayor Drapeau's grandiose schemes (which included buying the ocean liner *France* and turning her into a floating casino) and, finally, to alarm about the possible cancellation of the Games. When the Olympics were finally held, journalists tended to focus as much on the "concentration camp" aspect of the Olympic Village as on the Games themselves.

The news of November 15 actually made more waves in the foreign press than in the peaceful streets of Montreal. Outside Quebec, observers seemed stupefied by the results, but here, although no one had wanted to risk predicting it, it was the logical historical outcome.

1

The Liberal Machine Breaks Down

On October 18, 1976, Robert Bourassa plunged Quebec into a hasty election campaign two years before the end of his mandate. Officially, the Premier offered two reasons for going to the polls: constitutional negotiations with Ottawa, and labour relations in Quebec. But these official explanations are not really enough to account for the calling of the election, and the real reasons are to be found elsewhere.

One indication that there was more to the election than Bourassa let on comes from Ben Payeur, president of the Liberal party of Quebec. The election was, in Payeur's view, "a toss of the dice." According to Payeur, opinion polls commissioned by the Quebec Liberal party in the previous year had indicated a high degree of dissatisfaction with the government. And with each poll, the PQ was increasing its lead over the Liberals, while the Union Nationale (UN) was beginning to make its presence felt as well. Bourassa is a man of action, and didn't want to have his back against the wall; he always likes to take the initiative. If he had waited until 1977 to call an election, he would have risked being constantly on the defensive. And so he made his move, hoping that he would forestall the resurgence of the UN.

Of course the Quebec Liberals didn't release the results of their private opinion polls. And from the point of view of the public, the trend was less clear because, since 1974, what has been termed the "battle of the polls" had been in full swing. The two competing polling organizations were the Centre de Recherche sur l'Opinion Publique (CROP) and the Institut Québécois de l'Opinion Publique (IQOP). Early in 1976 they published contradictory results about the respective popularity of the two main contenders. CROP was accused of being infiltrated by Péquistes, while others pointed out that IQOP did surveys for the Liberal government. In the light of the results of November 15, when the PQ won forty per cent of the popular vote, it is certainly surprising that two weeks before the election IQOP was still giving the Liberals the lead. Probably if the polls that Payeur talks about had been published, the results of the election might have been a little less surprising.

During his first term of office between 1970 and 1973, Robert Bourassa made a number of highly controversial decisions. These included a contract awarded to Hilton Hotels for the Place Royale development in Quebec City, generous concessions to the multinational ITT-Rayonier on the North Shore, and one whose ultimate consequences have still not been measured — the James Bay project. In 1973, thanks to a fairly favourable overall economic situation and some strategic errors by the PQ, Bourassa received a mandate that was unprecedented in the history of Quebec: 102 members out of 110. But this crushing majority eventually produced problems of its own. The sixty or so Liberal backbenchers were left with time on their hands to cultivate their private and public vices. In fact, the impression left by the Bourassa government was one of carelessness with public funds, waste and a general lack of interest in people's problems and needs. And, although the integrity of the Premier and his cabinet was never in question, mismanagement, patronage and shady deals surrounded the government. The following are just some of the scandals that made newspaper headlines:

- *The Jean-Claude Boutin affair.* A Liberal MNA was accused of illegally acting as crown prosecutor at the same time that he was MNA for the riding of Johnson. The law forbids MNAs from receiving money from the government for professional services. Boutin was forced to resign.

- *The Gérard Shanks affair.* The MNA from St-Henri was accused of taking a sum of money from urban planner Roger Gagnon in exchange for exerting pressure on the Department of Municipal Affairs.

- *Government advertising contracts.* Most of these contracts were awarded to a well-known Montreal advertising agency which is also known for its leanings towards the Liberal party.

- *Tying up hot-lines.* The provincial Liberals admitted paying people to ask the ''right'' questions of various cabinet ministers invited to appear on radio hot-line shows.

- *The preferential list of lawyers.* Lawyers hired to defend certain government cases were found to be selected on the basis of their Liberal sympathies rather than professional competence.

- *The Guy Leduc affair.* According to testimony given to CECO, the Quebec government's inquiry into organized crime, the former MNA for Taillon had meetings in 1971 with persons identified with the Montreal underworld, including such well-known figures as Nicola Di Iorio and Frank Dasti.

- *The rotten meat story.* Certain government inspectors were found to have little enthusiasm for enforcing regulations preventing the sale of rotten meat for human consumption.

- *The Paragon affair.* The Premier's wife and her brother, a former cabinet minister, held twenty-four percent of the shares of a company that controlled a firm, Paragon, that supplied the government with its data-processing forms. As a result of this revelation the government was forced to adopt a code of conduct.

Besides the scandals, another cause of declining Liberal popularity was the government's tendency to look at issues and problems from a strictly administrative point of view. Bourassa saw his role, and that of his government, as a kind of social management, and he became caught up in purely day-to-day preoccupations. Both the government and the Liberal party became enveloped by this administrative viewpoint. Bourassa's platform offered nothing to inspire the electorate in terms of the future of Quebec, while the PQ was of course rousing its members and supporters with its vision of the possibilities for the future.

The big projects that Bourassa was involved with, such as James Bay and the Olympics, were liabilities rather than assets for the Liberals because of the way they had been carried out. The final result of these "monuments in concrete" seemed mainly to be lining the pockets of friends of the party. The Liberals' focus on administrative matters came up over and over again in the campaign; the party had little or nothing to offer in terms of policy in areas that required something more than simple administrative decisions. The result was that many social issues, such as the problems of old people, appeared to be at the very bottom of the list of government priorities, and there was even a certain attitude of contempt exhibited toward people on welfare and toward social issues such as health and medical care.

The result was that the Liberal party was unable to define itself clearly in voters' minds. Ben Payeur saw it this way: "Our party philosophy is as broad as the St. Lawrence." Bourassa would call himself a social democrat when he was addressing a group of workers, and a good capitalist when he was speaking to the Chamber of Commerce. For French-speaking Quebecers he was

Mayor Jean Drapeau (right) got Premier Robert Bourassa involved in his Olympic scheme.

a nationalist; for English-speaking Quebecers, a federalist. Bourassa tried to run on a consensus style of leadership: please everybody, annoy no one — or hardly anyone. The result was that no one knew where the Liberal ship was sailing and the natural result of that was that its captain's leadership capabilities were questioned.

The first person to do so openly was Jérôme Choquette. Choquette had served in the cabinet as Minister of Justice for five years. He was the architect of law reform measures that led to the creation of legal aid, small claims courts and compensation for victims of crime. He appeared to be one of the important ministers in Bourassa's cabinet, even to be one of the Premier's closest comrades in arms. In the summer of 1975 Choquette was shifted to the Department of Education — a suicidal post on the eve of a new school year which everyone knew would be politically very difficult. This decision was something of a surprise. Some political commentators wondered whether there might not have been an attempt to push him aside, whether this was really an attempt to get him out of the cabinet, for reasons that were then and have remained obscure. Two months later he did, in fact, resign from the cabinet and from the Liberal party as well.

What actually went on behind the scenes has not been revealed and likely won't be for some time to come. It was certainly more than a mere personality conflict or a divergence of views. Choquette himself has persistently refused to shed any light on the matter. His typical response to questioning has been: "You know, I just can't comment about that now." He has, however — strange as this may seem — appeared to retain a certain sympathy for Bourassa. He has even said, rather mysteriously, in reference to the former Premier, that "they poisoned him." But he has refused to identify "them."

Another signal of a realignment of forces within the Liberal

James Lorimer & Company, Publishers

Egerton Ryerson Memorial Building
35 Britain Street
Toronto, Canada M5A 1R7
(416) 363 8529

Review Copy

How Levesque Won, by Pierre Dupont

Translated by Sheila Fischman

136 pages   17 photographs

$5.95 paper/ $13.00 cloth

Publication date   January 31

Pierre Dupont will be available for interviews
in Toronto, Hamilton, Winnipeg, Calgary,
Edmonton and Vancouver during February. For
information, contact the following people:

February 14, Vancouver: McIntyre and Stanton,
    980-7086

February 15, Winnipeg: Mrs. Myrtle Lorimer,
    269-7437

February 16, Calgary: Kerry Longpre, 261-3070

February 17, Edmonton: Mary Mulhall, 488-2355

February 18, Toronto: Charlotte Sykes, 363-8529

Please send us two copies of your review.

Charlotte Sykes

party was an event that has not been well understood even though it is of considerable significance: the speech delivered by Prime Minister Trudeau, "Big Brother," to the provincial Liberal party convention in Quebec City on March 5, 1976. Trudeau was his usual charming, witty and polite self that evening, at this meeting of his Liberal colleagues. With the help of the wine, informality was the order of the day. Some days earlier Trudeau had set the tone for this encounter when, leaving dinner at Bourassa's, he had tried to avoid reporters' questions by saying that, in spite of everything, he'd had a good meal. To a second question, asking him how Bourassa was, he answered: "Yes, but apparently the only thing he eats is hot dogs." It was not long after the occasion of this gratuitous insult that Trudeau was standing up to speak, loosening his tie and undoing a couple of buttons on his shirt, ready to address the provincial Liberals. Here are a few of his comments about the Premier of Quebec:

> I have had the opportunity to read some of the resolutions to be presented to the convention in the next two days and I've seen that there are some rather difficult matters coming up, matters that will have to be discussed "eyeball to eyeball." The Premier of Quebec and I probably agree ninety-nine point nine per cent of the time; but there is that one-tenth of one per cent where we don't agree now, though we probably will eventually . . . But that's what's important when we talk about the constitution, when we squabble over the division of powers between the federal and provincial governments; and don't think that Quebec is the only province to want a new division of powers. That's why we haven't been able to resolve the constitutional problem over the past 100 years: if it was just Quebec and Ottawa it wouldn't take us long to come to an agreement . . . Let's say for instance if Bourassa and I were to squabble over a matter like having more power in the field of immigration and I said, okay, let's split it up, you've already got a fair amount of power in that area anyway; so

have I but you want more. Do you think the Queen of England's going to go and tell Bourassa: okay, Trudeau's right? Or that she's going to tell Trudeau, okay, Bourassa's the one that's right? Do you think the British government at Westminster is going to tell Quebecers: hang in there, we'll protect you against Ottawa? So you should understand this: when Bourassa and I have these discussions, things work out, maybe not very fast, but things work out . . . .

And you should understand that it's the nationalists, the separatists, that tell Bourassa: careful you don't fall into the trap. We're nationalists and we're keeping our eyes on you. And if you've got the nerve to bring the Constitution back to Canada you're going to have to answer to us . . . And so [on the subject of the predicted Olympic deficit] try to figure out what it meant when Drapeau and Bourassa and Rousseau said to me: you won't have to pay for the deficit if there isn't one and you won't have to pay for the deficit if it's small. But if it's a big one, then our thinking's going to change . . . I warned you that it'd be hard for me to explain to you. But think about it for twenty-four hours and you'll understand. I don't know if the Premier's going to understand it after twenty-four hours but give him two or three days and he'll figure it out . . . .

It's hard to think of any prime minister of Canada addressing a premier of Quebec in this fashion — especially when the two share the same political allegiance. Why did Trudeau feel he should denigrate his provincial counterpart? Was it just a gratuitous incident, or was it a sign of an intrusion by the federal party into the provincial Liberals' affairs?

Trudeau, however, wasn't the only one complaining about Bourassa. Within the provincial party itself at that time — and at the highest levels — there were already plans afoot to replace him as party leader. Ghislain Levasseur, an influential member of the party's Political Commission, presided over a secret committee that dealt with how this might be accomplished. Throughout the summer of 1976 this group was working very quietly toward its goal. An Olympic truce on party disputes required them to put up a harmonious appearance. It would have been strategically undesirable for them to get involved in any publicity just when representatives of the foreign press were in Montreal, looking for the slightest bit of interesting news.

In September and the first half of October, however, election rumours became more and more widespread. The announcement was finally made on October 18. Aside from the official reasons, Bourassa might very well have called the election because, well aware that he was in hot water, he wanted to put an end to these machinations to get rid of him and to strengthen his personal position and prestige within the party — and vis-à-vis Pierre Trudeau.

Indeed the image given off by the Liberal party after the election campaign began was one of lack of cohesion, disunity and warring factions. In fact all this had been visible for the previous year. According to Ben Payeur, Bourassa and his government had been under attack for a year at the party's various regional conventions: ''We felt as though we were at meetings of the Opposition.'' It was, of course, Bill 22 that served as the catalyst and stirred up factional warfare. This issue caused the two major factions within the party to come into conflict: the ''nationalists'' and the all-out federalists. But it would be a mistake to think that this was nothing more than a confrontation based on personal beliefs and choices. It was in fact a good deal more complex.

The key to the problem is found in the question: who is to control the exercise of government power in Quebec? Would it be people who wanted to subordinate it to the centralizing aims of the Trudeau government, or would it be held by those seeking

Trudeau meets Bourassa in 1975: a few months later he would publicly insult the Quebec premier.

more prerogatives for Quebec? At this particular point in the history of Quebec this question was far from being settled, and Premier Robert Bourassa found himself squeezed between the federalists à la Trudeau on the one side and the straightforward option of the Parti Québécois on the other. The political aim of Bill 22 was to maintain support for the Liberals within the English-speaking population while attempting at the same time to finesse the PQ; in the end the leader of the Liberal party succeeded only in clarifying the divisions within his own party through this difficult issue.

The election campaign served as a platform for these different groups. On one side were the "nationalists": men like Guy Saint-Pierre, Jean-Paul L'Allier, Jean Cournoyer, Denis Hardy and Ben Payeur. Bourassa has always been favourably inclined toward this group. But as leader of the government he couldn't let it show openly, and besides, it represented a minority position within the provincial party. Remarks that were disguised as jokes suggest the real views of members of this group. Ben Payeur: "If Quebec becomes independent one day it won't be the PQ that does it, it'll be us." Guy Saint-Pierre and Robert Bourassa had already said virtually the same thing, to everyone's amazement. And later, during the campaign, L'Allier declared to the Toronto magazine *Quest:* "The Liberal party would take Quebec out of Confederation if the federal government didn't concede certain powers to the provinces . . . The real threat to Canada doesn't come from our need to survive, but from a power-hungry, centralizing federal government." The Liberals were solidly opposed to any backing-off on the subject of Bill 22.

Some Liberal cabinet ministers, such as Jean Bienvenue, Lise Bacon, Claude Forget and Fernand Lalonde, looked at the Bill 22 controversy with one concern in mind: to be re-elected in their own ridings. The reason for their concern was very simple:

Bienvenue and Bacon had a high proportion of Italian voters in their ridings, which could make a difference in the results, while in Forget's and Lalonde's, there was a large English-speaking population. It was these ministers who forced Bourassa — who hadn't wanted to modify Bill 22 during the campaign — to change his mind in the face of the threat of an anti-Liberal vote. Jean Bienvenue, the Minister of Education, even threatened to resign if Bourassa didn't do so. Bourassa's reversal didn't in the end prevent the defeat of Lise Bacon and Jean Bienvenue. Even in the Liberal stronghold of Marguerite-Bourgeoys, Fernand Lalonde's majority was slashed from 13,000 to 1,000. Claude Forget had his margin cut in half from 1973. Voters seemed to have little love for Liberal ministers who chose to sit on the fence.

The federalists within the provincial Liberal party were a sizeable group. On the one hand there were the English-speaking members. We can leave aside George Springate, a kind of black sheep who was a source of embarrassment to nearly everybody in the party; the English-speaking leaders — William Tetley, Kevin Drummond, John Ciaccia and, particularly, Victor Goldbloom — were far more reserved and cautious in their public statements about Bill 22, as though they expected some imminent changes. None of them really managed to calm angry English-speaking voters, either because they lacked the capacity to do so or because they didn't want to. The situation was very different for French-speaking Liberals. Raymond Garneau, Jean-Noël Lavoie, Oswald Parent and Bourassa's *éminence grise,* Paul Desrochers — none of these men was able, or wanted, to set himself up as the champion of capitulation on Bill 22, or as the champion of a timid approach to the federal government.

In the midst of all of this two stars fell as though by chance from the Ottawa sky. They were to play out most thankless roles:

that of peacemaker in the English-speaking community and that of the sorcerer conjuring up the separatist threat in the French-speaking community. Bryce Mackasey was the man chosen for the first post, while the second went to the man once designated by Trudeau as "the minister responsible for Quebec," Jean Marchand. They were joined by one of the big guns of the federal Liberal organization, MP Roland Comtois, and André Raynauld, former Chairman of the Economic Council of Canada and one of Trudeau's chief economic advisers. After this mass candidate-parachuting operation had been carried out, René Lévesque, speaking with his usual frankness, described it as a "real South American-type putsch." He was indignant at the fact that "some ministers are in the process of finishing their careers as traitors to their people." While the provincial branch of the Liberal party risked disappearing without a trace, Bourassa looked more and more like a caretaker leader, as Jean Paré, editor of the magazine *l'Actualite,* put it.

Did this really amount to a putsch? One indication might be the conditions formulated by Mackasey and, particularly, by Marchand:

> • On the constitutional question, Marchand asked Bourassa to change certain positions that he had defended during the meeting of provincial premiers in Toronto.
> • On the language question, Marchand demanded a complete revision of Article 5 of Bill 22, in the direction of free choice.
> • On the question of labour relations in the public sector, Marchand advocated a limit on the right to strike.

The arrival of Marchand and Mackasey was negotiated at a very high level. Paul Desrochers played a key role in the exercise. The president of the provincial party himself admitted that "the negotiations were carried out over my head."

And just who is Jean Marchand? In the early sixties, when he was president of the Quebec Union Federation, the CNTU, he was brought in to work with the Lesage Liberals then in power in Quebec. Subsequently, he was one of the "three wise men" who went to Ottawa to establish "French power." Long known as Trudeau's right-hand man and as "number-two man" in Ottawa, he was the chief victim of the English-speaking backlash on the question of bilingualism. His prestige, however, remained intact in Trudeau's eyes. His continuing presence in Ottawa had probably become something of a nuisance for the Prime Minister, though, and Trudeau took comfort in the thought of Marchand's becoming his spokesman in Quebec City. Trudeau couldn't hope for a better representative than Marchand, who said during his campaign: "The French Canadians . . . are a small people. When one isn't six feet four — and, well, we aren't six feet four. We haven't got the numbers or the strength or the technology . . . ." This kind of statement was certainly enough to be disconcerting to even the most staunchly federalist Liberals in Quebec.

The federal Liberals had another reason to be annoyed with Bourassa. By choosing to launch his election campaign when he did, he dealt them a serious blow in a particularly sensitive area, that of campaign fund-raising. Before the provincial election was called the federal Liberals had, in fact, started their own fund-raising campaign. But the federal party's supporters had first of all to ensure the election of the provincial Liberals before coming to Trudeau's aid.

The effects of the attempt by the federal Liberals to put the provincial party into "trusteeship" during the campaign obviously unbalanced the Liberal machine in a number of ridings. Provincial Liberal organizers participated with little enthusiasm in the campaigns led by federal organizers. In the riding of

A defeated Bourassa announces his resignation as Quebec Liberal leader.

Louis-Hébert, for example, the big machine never really got into gear.

And as though all this wasn't enough for Bourassa, there seemed to be negative forces surrounding him and his government throughout the campaign. George Springate, his candidate in Westmount, described him as "the most hated and the most unpopular man in Quebec." The Liberal candidate in Kamouraska, J.M. Pelletier, told journalists that "there are a number of us who hope that there's going to be a good house-cleaning after the election and that some ministers will be kicked out or get themselves beaten." Pelletier even added, while speaking of how this could be done: "It seems to me that the way to do it would be to vote against the government." And there were some Liberal organizers in Montreal who kept repeating: "We're hoping for just one Liberal defeat — in Mercier [Bourassa's own riding]."

Things started to go badly for Bourassa on the very day the election was announced. He had sent a pre-recorded message to all radio and television stations, as he had done in 1973. But the head of the news department at Radio-Canada, Louis Martin, decided not to use the Premier's cassette. It was a good indication of the tension that existed between Bourassa and the press. A few days later his Finance Minister, Raymond Garneau, had the misfortune of not being able to hide the fact that the provincial deficit for 1976 would be more than one billion dollars.

On November 1, in the midst of the campaign, the employees of Hydro-Quebec went out on strike. The union, unable to reach an agreement with the managers of Hydro, had a few weeks earlier asked for Jean Cournoyer, Minister of Natural Resources, to act as mediator. The minister wanted to impose a solution that did not please the President of Hydro-Quebec and thus put Bourassa into an unneeded dilemma during an election campaign when he had lots of other problems to deal with. Bourassa, as was his habit, hesitated to come out for one side or the other; he was booed at meetings called by the striking employees, a fact that didn't help attract more people to campaign rallies. And once again he gave the impression of being a premier who couldn't make up his mind, who was powerless to make essential decisions.

Another strike that had electoral repercussions was the one at the Alcan plant in Arvida. Labour Minister Gérald Harvey, also the MNA for the region, was accused of concealing a report that blamed the company for having provoked the strike in order to sell off its inventory of excess production. The strikers made no attempt to conceal their anger throughout the Saguenay-Lac-St-Jean area and the consequences were disastrous both for the minister and for the government he represented.

A further disaster hit the Liberal campaign on November 4 when *Le Devoir* ran a front-page story on "how the Liberals had infiltrated the Quebec Liquor Board as of 1970." The newspaper's reporter had obtained confidential documents from CECO, the organized crime inquiry, that explained "how contracts, concessions, wine records and the list of official suppliers were selected by political figures and not by the directors [of the Liquor Board]." *Le Devoir* noted the names mentioned in the report, which included Paul Desrochers, special adviser to Premier Bourassa, and cabinet minister Raymond Garneau. The latter was quick to deny that he had committed any irregularity. Bourassa could only declare that "those are old stories, old stock," emphasizing that the whole matter was several years old. René Lévesque leaped to the occasion and made a statement on the matter:

> The CECO report on the Quebec Liquor Board described in detail a system of patronage and corruption that is used to finance

the Liberal party as well as to enrich its friends. This system corresponds to a kind of permanent extortion that might be compared with the underworld's system of protection: and in addition, it allows underworld elements to infiltrate and to carry out blackmail even in political circles.

Second, this is a system that can operate only with the collusion and active support of cabinet ministers and the highest authorities of the Liberal party.

Third, it is quite obviously the public that pays the expenses of this system, because the state is paying more for the goods and services which it purchases. It is a kind of fraudulent tax that is used to feed the party's coffers and its friends.

Fourth, and this is the most serious point, Mr. Bourassa has known about this file for at least fifteen months. He admitted himself, in the Assembly, that he had been informed about it at the very moment Jérôme Choquette, former Minister of Justice, had received the report in July.

The Parti Québécois members in the National Assembly tried to ascertain the truth from Mr. Bourassa and he accused them of trying to dirty reputations. It is clear now that Mr. Bourassa was deceiving the population as he has done on so many other occasions.

And the population will have the chance to let him know how they feel — about that and about so many other things — on November 15.

The Liquor Board file joined the file on Loto-Québec, into which CECO had also conducted an inquiry. CECO had brought to light a system for using the lottery to collect financial contributions to the Liberal party. A contribution was requested for the party from all those who held, or wished to obtain, a Loto-Québec franchise. It was learned that Liberal collectors had acquired as much as $40,000 in certain cases.

Scarcely five days before the November 15 election, a survey conducted by INCI (Institut de Cueillette de l'Information) for *Le Devoir,* the *Gazette,* the *Toronto Star,* and Radio-Mutuel predicted a decisive PQ victory, with fifty per cent of the popular vote. The shortest election campaign in the history of Quebec (twenty-eight days) was seen as leading to a major political reversal. Most observers remained skeptical. Still, one could imagine the possibility of a PQ government without really believing in it. By November 10, it was clear that the final result would go in one of two directions: 1) the voters would decide to teach Bourassa a lesson or 2) the population would become frightened and vote against the PQ thrust. The Liberal strategists, obviously running out of ideas, were counting on this second hypothesis.

And so the "fear machine" was put into high gear.

Among English-speaking and New Canadian voters the Liberal blitz took on a dramatic, in fact demagogic, aspect, appealing not to the mind but to the heart. The voters were asked to forget the "mistakes" of Bill 22, to forget about the sad record of the Bourassa regime. They were warned of the danger of voting Union Nationale: "No matter how we look at it, any split of the federalist vote plays into the hands of our real enemy, SEPARATISM." An appeal was made to what these voters identified with: Canada. When the Liberal commercial was run on English-language TV stations only the Canadian flag was shown at the beginning of the film, not the Quebec flag (while it was exactly the opposite on French television). Voters might have got the impression that it was Bryce Mackasey who was premier, because neither the name nor the picture of Robert Bourassa appeared in any of these messages. Apparently it had become absolutely impossible to sell him.

As the campaign progressed it also became clear that the executives of the English-language media had been mobilized to try to ensure the re-election of the Liberal Party in the largely

English-speaking West Island area of Montreal. This gave rise to two incidents worthy of note. The first took place at the Montreal daily, the *Gazette*. On November 13, the paper ran a signed editorial by its publisher, Ross Munro, that was an anguished appeal to those voters who lived in a riding where the PQ might get in, should the non-French-speaking vote be split. Munro spoke of a "calamity" if the PQ were to form the next government. But in the same edition of the paper, thirty-four journalists placed an ad disassociating themselves from the editorial, explaining that the important questions in the election campaign had to do with the way the government was running the province, not with independence. On CFCF, a radio station well known for its crusade against Bill 22, Don Martz, one of the station's owners, took the same stand as his colleague at the *Gazette*. John Robertson, well-known host of a CFCF hot-line program that had led the fight against Bill 22, refused to play the game and disassociated himself from his bosses. Death threats followed, and Robertson had to ask for police protection for three days, and even went into hiding on election day.

Another interesting aspect of the final days of the campaign was the off-handed admission of the Minister of Education, Jean Bienvenue, that he had sent a telegram to each of the Italian voters in his riding, Crémazie. The message, written in Italian, stated that voters couldn't "take the risk of losing what the Liberals have given us: old-age pensions, family allowances, medicare."

And finally, on election day itself, November 15, the *Montreal Star* reported that Charles Bronfman had declared that he would leave Quebec — taking his business operations and his baseball team along with him — if the PQ won the election. He had made these remarks the night before, while analysts were saying that the Jewish community seemed about to swing into the Union Nationale camp.

The Liberals also performed a last-minute sprint for the votes of French-speaking Quebecers by aiming not at their sentiments (as they had done with English-speaking voters) but at their pocketbooks. Full-page ads in the major newspapers — with no reference whatever to the Premier and the Liberal party itself not clearly identified — argued along the lines of: "We risk losing one of the highest standards of living in the world . . . or of dragging Quebec into the unknown, toward an inevitable separation from Canada. Their 'referendum' is an enormous electoral fraud in which the Péquiste leaders would control the results by manipulating a whole series of referendums in the same way that their trade-union allies have been manipulating strike votes." Elsewhere, Liberal campaign material claimed: "The trade unions' goons are René Lévesque's shock troops." Attempts were made among old people to persuade them that without Bourassa they'd have no more old age pensions, no more social peace. Federal Minister André Ouellet intervened to warn Quebecers about an eventual lowering of their standard of living, an end to subsidized oil prices and, to crown it all, the loss of freedom of speech. Ouellet also suggested that a PQ government would abolish elections for ten years. Evidently Bourassa and the Liberals didn't know which way to turn. It had become obvious that they would grab onto the smallest detail in the attempt to save their skins.

When it was announced that the Canadian dollar had dropped by 3/10 of one cent, Bourassa predicted that "Quebec runs the risk of losing its AA rating" with American investors, which would result in higher interest rates on foreign borrowing. Then he insisted that René Lévesque meet him again in order to debate the economic consequences of independence. Lévesque responded calmly: "It's a ridiculous invitation . . . we know that the Liberals are in the habit of making arrows out of any scrap of wood they turn up; but they're so desperate now they're using matches." Bourassa then accused Lévesque of cowardice for having turned down his invitation.

Bourassa ended his campaign by describing the PQ's campaign as an "intellectual hold-up." Trudeau's envoy, Jean Marchand, envisioned a future independent Quebec in these words: a "state of slavery in which most countries exist that have recently acquired their independence." He went on to give as an example the Uganda of Field Marshal Idi Amin. Finally, the Liberals turned on the news media as the last scapegoats for the collapse that seemed to be in the cards. Guy Godin, president of the provincial party for the Quebec City region, led the attack: "Yes, really, the news in Quebec has been prepared for a long time by a PQ fifth column that's infiltrated our newsrooms for years, and for the past three weeks they've been pulling out all the stops."

In this context, then, the stunning result of November 15 — from 102 members down to 26 for the Liberals — is not so surprising as it first appears. All the ingredients for a monumental defeat were there. Bourassa thought he would catch the other parties unprepared or, at the very least, stop their momentum. Most of his ministers had been opposed to his choice of election date; perhaps they were right, because a dozen of them lost their seats including some of the most important ones: the Minister of Labour (Gérald Harvey); the Minister of Natural Resources (Jean Cournoyer); the Minister of Agriculture (Normand Toupin); the Minister of Industry and Commerce (Guy Saint-Pierre); the Minister of Communications (Denis Hardy); the Minister of Co-operatives and Financial Institutions (Lise Bacon); the Minister of Cultural Affairs (Jean-Paul L'Allier); the Minister of

Education (Jean Bienvenue); and, most unusual of all, the Premier himself, Robert Bourassa.

Bourassa went to the polls to obtain a mandate for himself as premier and leader of the Liberal party, with the double aim of negotiating with Ottawa the eventual repatriation of the Canadian constitution and eliminating the separatist threat in Quebec. Ironically, the voters responded by posing the most serious threat yet offered to Canadian federalism.

2

The PQ Heads for Power

On the night of November 15 when René Lévesque, the new Premier of Quebec, said: "I didn't think I'd ever be so proud to be a Québécois," a thrill of excitement ran through the crowd at the Paul Sauvé Arena — and likely through most of the people watching the event on television too. It was a historic moment for two reasons: the people of Quebec had conquered a long-standing fear and, more important, they had just asserted themselves as a nation. It was the most powerful seismic shock recorded in Quebec in 1976, a total political upset: the PQ had moved up from six seats to seventy-one. One word can describe the atmosphere that prevailed from the beginning of that evening until the end: incredulity.

With eyes riveted to TV sets all over Quebec — and the rest of Canada — the mood was set a few minutes after the polls closed: the PQ leading in one seat. Then the figures started to climb: six seats, then seven; but in their homes, people remained skeptical: "It's just the east end of Montreal that's coming in now, the PQ's strong there." But then it jumped to ten, twenty, thirty, forty — and still people were cautious, repeating the same warnings, more hesitantly now, until the PQ was leading in seventy ridings.

With results piling in from every part of Quebec — la Mauricie, Gaspé, Abitibi, the Outaouais, the Quebec City area, even the largely English-speaking Eastern Townships — showing the PQ gaining everywhere, the results for greater Montreal still hadn't come in, and all kinds of speculations were swirling around. When the first results started coming in from ridings close to Montreal — Sauvé, Crémazie, Dorion, Mille-Iles — smokers were digging out their second packages of cigarettes (while the chain-smoking Lévesque was likely starting on his third). Then, a few minutes after 8:30 p.m., Bernard Derome, the solemn TV news-reader for Radio-Canada, announced that the PQ would form a majority government. And when the news broke that poet Gérald Godin had beaten ex-Premier Bourassa in the riding of Mercier, PQ supporters were ecstatic.

How did it all happen? It wasn't by magic that the PQ had overcome the various hurdles that had to be crossed before coming to power. Quebec nationalism started out as an emotional issue but it soon became a rational one. Nationalism came a long way from the days of the Ralliement pour l'Indépendance Nationale when a handful of people threw stones at the Confederation Train or picked fights in Murray's very English restaurants. And it came a long way from bombs in Westmount mailboxes and political kidnappings as a means to have political communiqués read over national television; by 1976, the time for such desperado tactics was long past. The PQ persuaded people who favoured an independent Quebec that they would have to build their new society with the aid of a political instrument — the Parti Québécois. It was the bet that René Lévesque had accepted in 1967 when he founded the Mouvement Souveraineté-Association, which led to the creation of the Parti-Québécois a year later. The PQ got twenty-three per cent of the popular vote (seven seats) in 1970; in 1973, it was thirty per

The air was electric in the Paul Sauvé Arena when Premier-elect Lévesque
made his entrance the night of November 15.

cent and six seats; on November 15, 1976, seventy seats — and power.

The Popular Vote						
	1970		**1973**		**1976**	
	Votes	Seats	Votes	Seats	Votes	Seats
PQ	662,404 (23%)	7	897,309 (30%)	6	1,275,335 (40%)	71
Liberals	1,304,341 (45%)	72	1,623,734 (55%)	102	1,076,233 (34%)	26
UN	564,544 (20%)	17	146,209 (5%)	—	590,841 (19%)	11
Créditistes	321,370 (10%)	12	294,706 (10%)	2	156,786 (5%)	1
Others	20,311 (1%)	—	8,520 (0%)	—	64,556 (2%)	1
Total	2,872,970(100%)	108	2,970,478(100%)	110	3,163,751(100%)	110

It was in 1974 that the PQ's aspirations to achieve power began to be taken seriously. Expectations had been too high at the time of the 1973 election and the party wasn't really ready yet: the instrument lacked precision. Bourassa and his election specialists treated the PQ as a joke and the demoralized PQ organization fell apart after the election. The party strategists had to revise their methods. The September 1974 fund-raising campaign allowed them to experiment. They were aware that the most serious shortcoming in the previous election had been in the party's organization and so they concentrated on restructuring it. Response to the fund-raising campaign was favourable and the process was speeded up. To begin with Lévesque was provided with an adequate staff for the first time. A full-time chief organizer, Michel Carpentier, was appointed. Then the party was decentralized and local organizations set up in the various regions of Quebec. The people in charge of the regions were joined by other organizers who had worked in the past for the old parties and were now prepared to share their experience. These former Liberals and Union Nationale organizers gave the party a more professional touch.

Another and perhaps more important change, in the light of the results of November 15, was the inclusion in the party platform of a plank promising that a referendum would be held before a declaration of Quebec independence. The resolution, moved by Claude Morin at the PQ's national convention in 1974, provoked an impassioned controversy within the party but it also led to an appreciable increase in the number of its supporters. Morin, who was subsequently nicknamed "the father of *étapisme*," the word used to designate the one-step-at-a-time approach to independence, said: "Quebec must make each move at the proper time, one move at a time . . . the first step is to change governments." This was the key that would help let the PQ get past doors that had previously been closed to it. In 1973, Bourassa had managed to frighten the electorate by talking about "the adventure of independence," thereby avoiding any debate on his government's record. The 1976 election was another matter. The Liberal "election makers" tore their hair out trying to discredit the PQ's new idea, which Ben Payeur himself described jealously as "the find of the century."

In 1973, the PQ began to emphasize a more diversified membership as well. Fund-raising campaigns also served as recruiting drives, and members were sought from all levels of society. Before the election, there were 85,000 members in the party; these included about twenty-five percent who were over sixty-five, as well as students, intellectuals, small businessmen, professionals, union leaders, workers, journalists and farmers. More than fifty per cent were women and their energy and zeal contributed greatly to the party's success. People from all these groups first came to the PQ because of its democratic image. Ordinary members found they had more of a chance to be heard than in any of the traditional political parties in Quebec. And, of course, people were also attracted by the vision of the future offered by the Parti Québécois. They liked its social-democratic platform, a welcome departure from the Bourassa-Drapeau-

Trudeau style of economic "liberalism." The image of a "clean" party, with "clean" coffers as well, added to the attractiveness of this new political force. The PQ is, in fact, the only party ever to have come to power in Quebec financed only by its members and sympathizers. Lévesque is adamant on this point: "The PQ is condemned to be poor but we're proud of it." And the party members appreciate this and respect Lévesque's integrity.

This, then, was the combination of ingredients that made the Parti Québécois ready to fight an election a year before it was finally announced on October 18. If Bourassa thought he had taken his adversaries by surprise he was sadly disappointed. It is more likely that Bourassa was aware of how things stood inside the PQ and rushed into a premature election out of fear of a putsch within his own party.

Throughout the campaign it was the PQ that kept the initiative. Never at any point was it put on the defensive. The Liberals wanted the debate to focus on the question of independence, as it had in 1973, but the PQ strategists forced Bourassa to defend his government and his "projects". He was attacked on grounds of effectiveness and integrity. While Bourassa was struggling desperately to keep up appearances, Lévesque was blithely travelling across the province delivering his message. During an hour-long speech he would spend fifteen minutes criticizing the government, fifteen minutes talking about PQ solutions and the remaining time explaining that Quebec would become independent only after long reflection, followed by a democratically conducted referendum.

Lévesque did his best to be as reassuring as possible, carefully avoiding too frequent references to the language question and to independence. He avoided the kind of monster rallies that might have scared people off by making the party look too powerful,

Lévesque was the only PQ ''star'' to get province-wide exposure.

and throughout the campaign he went out of his way to minimize the party's real strength. For example, when the INCI poll came out a few days before the election, giving the PQ a clear majority, he deliberately sent out word that it wasn't wise to be too optimistic. Obviously, he didn't want exaggerated optimism to slow down the campaign and he particularly didn't want the party workers to cut back their efforts: everything had got off to such a good start that a last-minute slowdown had to be avoided.

The PQ campaign strategy left nothing to chance, except perhaps on one point, the question of the referendum. They had decided to raise the question only to reply to Bourassa's attacks on "the PQ's real intentions." They would let Bourassa attack and, in effect, give him enough rope to hang himself. Then Lévesque would make this observation: "What scares me is that the Bourassa government might be elected for another four years. If that happens, I don't know if Quebec could be put together again." Obviously this had an effect. People asked themselves whether Bourassa was capable of governing when he hadn't been able to do an adequate job even with 102 out of 110 members. The PQ never allowed Bourassa to take the offensive. One by one, it threw his government's scandals, weaknesses and poor administration in his face — and there was no shortage of ammunition. This was the context for the PQ's main campaign slogans: *We need a real government, Quebec needs a real leader.*

It took strict discipline to stick to the established plan. The "stars" of the party had only one role to play — to win in their own ridings. Union Nationale leader Rodrigue Biron had set the tone for his campaign by telling his troops to "beat the Liberals, riding by riding," just as Daniel Johnson had done in 1966. But his troops were, to say the least, poorly prepared and few in number. The PQ, on the other hand, did precisely what Biron had hoped to accomplish. Only Lévesque was thrown into the "national" limelight. The PQ leader, who has been called "the man who is most devoted to the interests of the people of Quebec," went from riding to riding, meeting with small groups of active members to give them the good word.

Lévesque's gestures, his disarming familiarity (in contrast with Bourassa's technocratic style) and, most of all, his easy way of chatting (with the ever-present cigarette and cup of coffee) make him, at times, almost irresistibly convincing. He juggles words and phrases and clichés — and his talent for sticking pins in his adversaries is unequalled in Quebec politics. Take his description of Jean Marchand, for example: "a drowning man clutching a shaky raft." To his opponent in the riding of Taillon, who in predicting a third defeat for Lévesque quoted the proverb "Three always follows two," his response was: "Wise men invent proverbs; idiots repeat them." Throughout the election campaign, he kept describing Bourassa as "the outgoing Premier" and his government as "the outgoing government."

Aside from the "find of the century" (the referendum), the PQ took the Liberal machine by surprise with its series of promises on questions that — as the party never hesitated to point out — were of more concern to the voters than the tower for the Olympic Stadium. But it wasn't just these promises that threw the Liberals off balance; it was the way they were presented to the electorate. The PQ was very careful to spread them out over the entire twenty-eight-day campaign. By doing so they were able to hold the attention of the media day after day, while forcing Bourassa to launch a counter-attack in every case. When Bourassa did, Lévesque would ask him: "And what has your government done in this area?" There was an obvious advantage to not presenting all the promises at one stroke — it ensured that the bill wasn't too high at any one time.

• To begin with, the PQ undertook to publish its election expenses *before* the end of the campaign. This promise was kept on November 11, when the PQ published a report in all Quebec's French-language dailies:

Rapport des revenus
et dépenses électorales nationales du Parti Québécois
au 11 novembre 1976

Revenus

Réserve électorale au début		$200,000.	
Contributions des associations de comté du Parti		50,000.	$250,000.

Revenus perçus entre le 18 octobre et le 11 novembre 1976

	Nombre	Montant net	
Cartes de membre	29,605	$72,267.	
Dons	14,997	318,298.	
	44,602		
			390,565.
Total			$640,565.

Notes: La moyenne des dons est de $21.22
46 dons sont supérieurs à $250.00, dont 10 entre $1,000. et $2,500.
Conformément aux règlements du Parti Québécois aucun don supérieur à $250.00 ne provient de compagnies, associations ou syndicats.
9 dons totalisant $15,000. sont sous examen quant à leur conformité avec les règlements du Parti. 8 de ces dons se situent entre $1,000. et $2,500.
Aucun don ne dépasse la somme de $2,500.

Dépenses électorales

Factures acquittées	$405,899.	
Factures à payer	48,590.	
Dépenses engagées	168,492.	$622,981.

Rapport des vérificateurs
Nous avons examiné les documents comptables relatifs aux revenus et dépenses électorales nationales du Parti Québécois pour la période du 18 octobre au 11 novembre 1976. Notre examen a comporté une revue générale des procédés comptables et des contrôles ainsi que les sondages des régistres et autres preuves à l'appui que nous avons considérés nécessaires dans les circonstances.

À notre avis les chiffres donnés ci-haut représentent fidèlement les opérations financières du Parti Québécois relatives à l'élection en cours.

[signature]

Brisson, Guérin, Grenier, Lalonde & Ass., C.A.

Montréal, le 11 novembre 1976

Lévesque and MNA Claude Charron congratulate each other.

• On October 28, Dr. Denis Lazure (now Minister of Social Affairs) stated: "The PQ advocates establishing a ceiling on medical fees under the Medical Act and replacing them by salaries. To accomplish this it will first be necessary to make the incomes of doctors on salary more attractive relative to those who are remunerated by fees. The present difference is enormous."

• The same day, in Sept-Iles, René Lévesque promised:
— free drugs for people sixty-five and over;
— free dental care for children under eighteen;
— inclusion of chiropractic care under Medicare;
— free hospital transport.

• On November 11, the twenty candidates in the Montreal area promised:
— a definitive halt to work on the city's controversial east-west autoroute;
— a strengthening of local power through the creation of elected neighbourhood councils;
— public transportation as a priority;
— a public housing policy;
— a public inquiry into Montreal's municipal administration and into the Olympics.

• On November 12, Marcel Léger promised that the PQ would transform Ile Ste-Thérèse, just off the extreme east end of Montreal Island, into an enormous public park, twice the size of Montreal's Botanical Gardens, the municipal golf course and Mount Royal Park combined. This would fall within the framework of a program to turn unused lands on the St. Lawrence into parks.

• On October 27, René Lévesque promised that once the PQ formed the government, he would establish an automobile insurance scheme, accessible to everyone. A board would be established to deal with rates and claims. The scheme would include private insurance companies, which would continue to provide complementary services.

- On November 10, the PQ leader promised a program to assist small and medium-sized businesses in Quebec. This special aid program would be tailored to encourage the development of those industries based on the subcontracting of specialized products and linked with a policy of purchasing in the public and para-public sectors that would strongly favour firms operating in Quebec. He estimated that this new purchasing policy would inject an additional $400 million into the Quebec economy in the first year.

- On November 13, Jacques Couture spelled out how the PQ program would apply to the Montreal Urban Community. He advocated decentralization and financial autonomy. The MUC and the City of Montreal would assume responsibility for housing and urban development. Property taxes would be eliminated under a program of fiscal reform. Couture promised that public housing would be built for the elderly and poor: this would also constitute a housing pool for flood victims. He promised to reduce the demolition of existing dwellings to a minimum, and to encourage renovation and rehabilitation of buildings. A PQ government would also conclude an agreement with the City of Montreal to set up a large co-operative housing project in the Domaine St-Sulpice, a vast undeveloped area in north-end Montreal that the city bought from the Sulpician Fathers.

- On November 13, Lévesque described the James Bay Project as "the finest example of governmental mismanagement." He went on: "What is needed at James Bay is tight control over costs, something the PQ will establish once it is in power. There's no question of stopping the work, but it is essential to revise the timetable so that the work would be carried out at a rate that corresponded to Quebec's energy needs and, more important, to its financial capacity.''

● On October 25, Lévesque attacked Bill 22 as discriminatory. He promised to reinstate freedom of choice in the language of instruction for the children of immigrants already living in Quebec. New immigrants, however, would be obliged to send their children to French-language schools during their first five years in Quebec.

● On October 29, Lévesque offered his solutions in the area of safety on the job: in the short term, to apply existing laws which were not respected by employers, and in the long term, to reform the Workmen's Compensation Commission. He emphasized the importance of giving workers' representatives responsibility for overseeing working conditions.

● On October 29, Camille Laurin promised to improve the lot of old people by ''eliminating the money wasted by the Liberal party on favouritism, patronage, corruption and fancy deals; this money would be used instead to set up a network of home nursing services and meals on wheels for senior citizens''; in addition, priority would be given to free public transportation in the cities and to reduced fares for inter-city travel for senior citizens.

In themselves, these election promises constitute a pretty full program. There is, of course, no question of keeping all of them in the first session, but the Lévesque government will have to get down to it if it doesn't want to be accused of incompetence. According to its leader, the Parti Québécois committed itself to an ''intentionally'' demanding program; ''the hope that it arouses mustn't be disappointed.'' The voters elected it to form ''a good government'' and that's its first task. How it carries out its program will be seen as a test of whether it can lead Quebec to independence.

The PQ profited from some unexpected but tremendously valuable support in the form of an editorial in the November 12 issue of the influential daily *Le Devoir,* signed by that paper's august publisher, Claude Ryan. He dismissed the Liberals, whom he considered to be incapable of governing, and supported the Parti Québécois to whom he attributed five "qualities" which made them, in his eyes, "suitable to aspire to power." Those qualities are: 1) its structures and open financing; 2) the qualities of its leader; 3) its success in integrating young people into the political process; 4) the merits of a competent, honest team; and 5) the PQ's noble vision of public life. The following day, however, Ryan reminded his readers of his "objections to independence," emphasizing the "absence of formal guarantees" on the whole question of the referendum. One may wonder whether Ryan's new approach — he had previously supported the Liberals — had anything to do with the demise of the pro-independence daily *Le Jour,* which during its brief life had given *Le Devoir* some stiff competition in sales and readership. In fact the PQ had done *Le Devoir* a favour — albeit unintentional — by voluntarily and prematurely putting an end to *Le Jour*. Patrice Laplante, the PQ candidate who defeated Lise Bacon in the riding of Bourassa, has said: "The PQ voluntarily let *Le Jour* go under. The decision was made two months before it closed down. The paper wasn't serving the interests of the party — there were too many radical journalists working for it. *Le Jour* would have been damaging to the PQ's campaign."

One of the crowning glories on November 15 was unquestionably the victory of Gérald Godin — former editor of the defunct left-wing weekly *Québec-Presse,* editor-in-chief of the left-wing publishing house *parti pris,* and poet into the bargain —

who took the riding of Mercier away from Robert Bourassa. The population of this working-class riding in the heart of Montreal is seventy-five per cent French-speaking. Bourassa, a native of the parish of St-Pierre Clavet in the riding — but a resident of posh Outremont — had represented it since 1966. One story has it that an influential Liberal of the time had suggested to Bourassa that he run in Mercier "so that he could get closer to the people." This Liberal was none other than René Lévesque.

In this last campaign not even the prestige that should go along with being leader of the government was able to prevent Bourassa's defeat. Even his family had to come to the rescue: his son played guitar at meetings, and his wife was reported to have gone door-to-door along Laurier Street — accompanied by two "gentlemen," while the chauffeur of her limousine waited impatiently. Toward the end of the campaign, some Liberal workers in Mercier, fearing the defeat of their leader, went so far as to phone voters in the name of the Parti Québécois, trying to frighten them with suggestions along this line: "I'm calling on behalf of the PQ. We hear you're going to be voting for us — that'll be quite a revolution!"

As for the PQ, it had only one goal in Mercier: victory. The party's 500 members in the riding hadn't taken into account their adversary's tangible assets: he had the advantage of widespread national publicity. But Godin had the edge in the local publicity; his posters were everywhere, in windows and hanging from balconies. He followed to the letter the time-tested NDP and PQ tactic of working patiently and methodically, street by street and house by house, visiting no fewer than 6000 homes. When the announcement was read out at the Paul Sauvé arena on election night: "Godin, Mercier, elected," the place erupted in frenzy. His victory was a symbol of the fact that the keynote of the campaign — organization — had resulted in an unequivocal success.

Candidate Lévesque addresses a meeting in his riding of Taillon.

3

The "Resurrection" of the Union Nationale?

Was the soul of Maurice Duplessis still watching over the destiny of the Union Nationale's old blue machine in 1976? When newly-elected leader Rodrigue Biron urged his troops to beat the *rouges* (or "reds" as the Liberals have been traditionally known in Quebec, while the Tories and Union Nationale were called the *bleus* or "blues") riding by riding, he sounded strangely like "le chef" in his heyday.

When the Liberals barely scraped into office in 1960, putting an end to the twenty-year domination of Quebec public life by Maurice Duplessis and his lieutenants — a period commonly referred to as "Quebec's dark ages" — newly-elected Premier Jean Lesage acknowledged his victory by proclaiming: "We've beat the big blue machine." The machine had been synonymous with patronage, corruption, paternalism and, at election time, such devices as buying votes, "selective" road paving, strong-arm tactics and mud-slinging campaigns. It was in these good old days when parish priests preached sermons to the faithful: "Heaven is blue and Hell is red."

After Lesage's victory, it was generally thought that these tactics were at an end, but the Union Nationale stayed around and was returned to power in 1966. Daniel Johnson, the new leader, tried to transform the party but the old guard was still hanging in. After Johnson's death, his successor, Jean-Jacques Bertrand, was shown to be incapable of solving the language problem (he tried with Bill 63, the predecessor to Bill 22), a trap that caught more than one politician. In 1970, with the revival of the Liberal party under the leadership of ''a brilliant young economist,'' and with the first participation in the electoral scramble by the Parti Québécois, the UN, exhausted, gave up the struggle and won scarcely twenty per cent of the popular vote. Its dizzying fall continued in 1973, under the leadership of Gabriel Loubier who, by directing his energies mainly at the ''separatist'' threat rather than at the government, managed to have not a single member elected and picked up only five per cent of the popular vote. Observers were already hammering nails into the Union Nationale's coffin, sending it on to join Duplessis, its founder, in purgatory.

It didn't work out quite that way. A by-election was called in the rural Eastern Townships riding of Johnson in August 1974 when Liberal MNA Jean-Claude Boutin was forced to resign and Maurice Bellemare, a former Duplessis lieutenant, managed to get himself elected. His goal was to disinter the UN and turn it into a third political force in Quebec. Bellemare considered his role a temporary one and worked toward a leadership convention that would choose a new, young leader capable of restructuring the party and breathing new life into it.

Meanwhile, the remnants of Yvon Dupuis's Parti Présidentiel joined the ranks of the UN rather than returning to the Créditistes from whom they had split off. The executive of the Parti Présidentiel became members of the UN executive, including Clément Patrie, who would play a part in subsequent events. Other former Créditistes, such as Phil Cossette, Dr. Jean-Marie

Côté and Yvon Brochu, became very influential at various levels of the party.

These events took place in November 1975. Four months later, members of the UN in Montreal were invited to an informal meeting to discuss the leadership question. The organizers asked them what they thought of Rodrigue Biron as the new leader. Their response was: Rodrigue who? The man responsible for this discovery was one of the Créditiste big guns in the riding of Lotbinière.

Bellemare and the UN old boys were also on the lookout for a new leader. Their choice was Jacques Tétreault, former mayor of the Montreal suburb of Laval. Each clan had its candidate, then, and everything was set for the May 1976 convention.

People were quick to note that the next leader would be the one with the most money to hand out. An old party member from Sept-Iles offered an account of what went on. Bursting with pride at being at another Union Nationale convention — because he'd been at lots since the days of Duplessis — he went to this one thanks to the generosity of the Rodrigue Biron organization. They paid for his transportation, his hotel room, his meals — and offered a $200 bonus if he voted wisely. He was quick to realize that it was profitable to be seen wearing a variety of candidates' badges. His roommate, for instance, was proudly flaunting his Biron button the first morning — and that same evening he had traded it for a Tétreault badge, only to come back the following morning boosting Biron again. There is no point in trying to understand all the machinations — but it seemed that the Biron side was usually leading. Reliable sources estimate that the winner spent around $200,000. One of the fine old Duplessis traditions had made a comeback.

The new forty-one-year-old leader is the son of a small-town industrialist. There is no Union Nationale tradition in the family:

Unknown six months before the election, Rodrigue Biron saved the Union Nationale from oblivion.

the father is a staunch Liberal, another son a militant Péquiste who during the campaign told anyone who wanted to listen: "I'm working against my brother." His first task was to attempt to put together a third political force in Quebec, which meant joining forces with Jérôme Choquette, Fabien Roy and their supporters who had come together to form the Parti National Populaire (PNP). Biron, the neophyte, lost no time in stamping the party with his own style, which was quick to show up in the delicate negotiations that began shortly after. A first-hand observer of these negotiations provides the following account:

Last June 24, the party executive held a meeting at the Queen Elizabeth Hotel in Montreal to discuss the negotiations that were underway with the Parti National Populaire. Before the executive tackled this question they turned to current affairs, at the special request of Mr. Biron. It was decided to change the party's constitution to make room on the executive for Fernand Grenier, former president of the UN and a good friend of Mr. Biron's. This was done under the pretext that a former president should automatically be part of the new executive in order to help the new president carry out his tasks. After this hand had been played they moved on to the question of the negotiations. It was agreed that nothing would be decided before the fall.

The executive, however, was called to an emergency meeting on August 3, at the Auberge des Gouverneurs in Ste-Foy, just outside Quebec City. To the surprise of several members, it was announced that an agreement had been signed between the UN and the PNP concerning the terms and conditions for an eventual fusion. However, Mr. Choquette had been led to believe that the UN executive would have to accept the agreement before it was put into effect. Messrs. Bellemare, Cloutier and Vincent came to talk with the members of the executive during the coffee-break. Bellemare, with his usual verve, offered this bit of advice: "Maybe it isn't such a good thing if the whole executive agrees.

The papers will say we want Choquette at any price." Biron continued: "The main thing is to have him. He'll be easy to manipulate. And if he doesn't work, we kick him out. That still wouldn't keep us from hanging on to Roy and his executive and his members." Michel Côté, party President and long-time enemy of Choquette, was not present at this meeting; he was in Haiti for a month's vacation.

The session resumed. The fourteen people present voted in favour of the agreement. However, when it came to the terms and conditions, eight voted for and six against. This was for the sake of appearances, because it was important that "the executive shouldn't be in complete agreement." Grenier then phoned Drummondville, where Choquette and Roy were in a motel room, waiting for the answer. Roy answered the phone; Grenier told him that the discussion was still going on but that "there's a good chance that we'll accept you." Later, Biron told us: "Choquette wants to change the name of the UN and he insists on a leadership conference. He wants too much. But we were smart enough not to mark it down in the agreement." Robert Charette even added that Choquette "is intellectually lazy; he can't even read an 8-1/2 x 11 document. He doesn't like work — he gives it to other people to do. He wants to be the leader, with all the fanfare. We'll be able to manipulate him; he's a bloody nothing." Next the executive gave Clément Patrie the mandate to negotiate with the "nothing."

The last meeting that was held on the subject took place on September 2, at the Dauphin Motel in Drummondville. Michel Côté was back from his holidays. Nothing was working between the UN and the PNP. They accused one another of every kind of sin in the presence of journalists. The PNP's negotiating committee was also at the motel; its members were in the next room, waiting for the executive's decision. Biron began the session by saying: "We've got to find a way to get rid of Choquette." The discussion continued for several hours, while Choquette's emissaries cooled their heels. From time to time they looked through the glass door to see if we were finished. When we decided not to merge with the PNP, Michel Côté advised Patrie: "Don't tell them, let them wait. They'll go away on their own." From then on whenever one of them came to have a look at what was going on the others started laughing. They left that night at eleven o'clock, very upset. Biron and the others were roaring with laughter . . . When Choquette phoned that night Patrie demanded the PNP's membership list by noon, otherwise the UN would cancel the agreement. Obviously it was impossible to meet this demand.

There was no coming together of Jérôme Choquette and the Union Nationale for the upcoming election.

Some PNP and UN members like to think that if Choquette had been leader of the UN or one of its main standard-bearers, the party would have done better. A look at the total votes for the two parties does not support this: the PNP got 30,000 (less than one per cent of the popular vote) and the UN 600,000 (nineteen per cent). A coherent third political force might have inspired even more voters to leave the Liberal party, but that is not certain. It's hard to conceive of the co-existence within a single party of men with as little mutual esteem as Roy and Grenier, Choquette and Biron, or Choquette and Michel Côté. Côté had been the head of the City of Montreal's legal department and a close associate of Mayor Drapeau's for many years. It is well known that since October 1970, there has been an unconcealed hatred between him and Choquette. During the October Crisis, Côté had advocated a hard line while Choquette, despite his tough image at the time, didn't want to go as far. Côté was also the sponsor of most of the City of Montreal's controversial bylaws, such as the one prohibiting demonstrations and the one that removed newspaper vending machines from the city's streets. Choquette says of him

Unification Agreement between the Union Nationale and the Parti National Populaire

1. The Union Nationale and the Parti National Populaire, through the will of their respective leaders and executives, agree to unite their movements within a single alliance with the goal of providing Quebecers with a political force capable of representing their individual and collective aspirations, and of translating their national ideal into reality;

2. Messrs. Jérôme Choquette and Rodrigue Biron and the executives of the Parti National Populaire and of the Union Nationale agree to combine their efforts to prepare and bring about the fusion of their parties with a view to presenting a team capable of governing the affairs of Quebec;

3. There is hereby established a technical committee of ten (10) persons, composed of five (5) representatives of each of the two parties. The mandate of this committee is to prepare and hold a convention for fusion, organization and orientation, which will be held in Montreal on October first, second and third, nineteen hundred and seventy-six (1976);

4. This committee may, if necessary, form sub-committees;

5. The question of the name of the alliance will be put before those attending the convention which will make the decision on the matter;

6. A constitution will also be adopted by the convention;

7. The leadership of the alliance will be assumed jointly by Messrs. Rodrigue Biron and Jérôme Choquette. Monsieur Jérôme Choquette will assume responsibility for policies and program. Monsieur Rodrigue Biron will assume responsibility for administration and organization;

8. Messrs. Maurice Bellemare, Jérôme Choquette, Fabien Roy will constitute the parliamentary wing of this alliance. Monsieur Maurice Bellemare will be the parliamentary chief and Monsieur Fabien Roy the parliamentary leader;

SIGNED* at Drummondville, this twenty-ninth day of July, nineteen hundred and seventy-six (1976) and SUBJECT to ratification by the executives of the two parties.

Rodrigue Biron
Leader of the Union Nationale

Jérôme Choquette
Leader of the
Parti National Populaire

Fernand Grenier

Fabien Roy

---

* At the bottom of the document are affixed the signatures of Messrs. Rodrigue Biron, Jérôme Choquette, Fernand Grenier and Fabien Roy.

that he is "a dangerous man." With Côté as president of the Union Nationale, Choquette's chances of getting anywhere within the party were very small. There are those who question Côté's motives for joining the party's ranks. Some members of the executive say that he had to leave his job with the City of Montreal because of his role in certain controversial issues — the Olympics, for example. It's interesting to note, in this respect, that during the parliamentary hearings on the Olympics, Maurice Bellemare opposed a judicial inquiry into the games.

In any case, these same people say that Côté wanted to run for the UN leadership, but that he had arrived on the scene too late to have any reasonable chance of getting in. He will be waiting for a while, then, unless Biron doesn't last very long.

But it's hard to foresee Biron stepping down for some time yet, especially after the outcome of the November 15 election. The UN leader had set himself two objectives during the campaign: to beat the *rouges* and give the UN a new electoral base. To some degree, he achieved his goal. The UN did elect eleven members, all in ridings formerly held by Liberals. During the campaign, Biron's bubbling optimism, which led him to predict that he would win sixty seats, may have been appropriate to the occasion but it wasn't quite realistic. Still, the UN is at least back to where it was in 1970, and far ahead of where it was in 1973, when it got only five per cent of the vote and elected no members. The night of November 15, the UN organizers were jubilant. They had, in fact, accomplished what they had set out to do twenty-eight days earlier. They had got back a large portion of their traditional support in the Eastern Townships, as well as becoming the second party for New Canadian voters and the largely English-speaking population of the West Island of Montreal. The victory of William Shaw in Pointe-Claire, the most heavily Anglo-Saxon riding in Quebec (eighty-five per cent) is significant.

Forty years after English voters had helped Duplessis overturn the corrupt Liberal régime of Godbout, the UN had regained a certain favour in Quebec's English-speaking community.

There is however a danger that these new supporters will give Mr. Biron some problems. How can he reconcile the contradictory interests of the old nationalist UN voters in the Eastern Townships with the English-speaking voters who chose his party as a reaction against the creeping separatism of Robert Bourassa? The UN old guard certainly didn't come back to the party expecting to hear that children in Quebec should be gradually anglicized, nor did English-speaking UN voters expect to be told that French is Quebec's only language. During the campaign Biron tried to please everybody in order to get votes. Such political opportunism may yield certain short-term dividends, but there is a risk of damaging party unity in the long term.

Most commentators noted that the UN election material changed tone depending on the audience it was aimed at. Biron personally instructed the telephone operators at the UN's headquarters on Berri Street in Montreal to tell French-speaking callers that French would be the official language of Quebec under a UN government — and to tell English-speaking callers that there would be two official languages. He saw no contradiction in this but members of his party may have been more alert to the possibility of one.

"Anything goes as long as it brings in the votes," Biron kept telling his organizers. He had the same approach to the whole problem of bilingual air traffic control. In private he said that Les Gens de l'Air, the French-speaking pilots and controllers, were "behind the times," while on French-lanugage radio station CKAC he promised to defend them if he was elected.

It was Biron's personal style to forge alliances between groups that were, to say the least, different. For example, to deal with

English-speaking Montrealers he ueed federal Conservative organizers. In Westmount, it was Egan Chambers, a former Tory MP. Dr. Shaw, who would be elected in Pointe-Claire, is a supporter of the ultra-conservative former mayor of Moncton, Leonard Jones. These Conservatives even admit that they met Biron well before the UN leadership convention, and were satisfied with him.

It should be remembered that for the past six years the federal Conservatives have been toying with the idea of forming a provincial party in Quebec. Biron seems to have convinced them to do nothing, to let him handle things. Clément Vincent, one of the main UN organizers, used his ties with the Conservatives to support Biron's position. Biron was assured of around sixty per cent of the vote in Montreal's Italian community because of his plan to reinstate freedom of choice in the language of education, hearkening back to Bill 63. But it's hard to see how he could get the Italians to work in the future with his mélange of Knights of Columbus and Créditistes.

The Knights of Columbus, a semi-secret Christian society which represents the interests of small businessmen and of which Biron used to be Canadian president, supported its former leader in several ridings. Thirty members of the organization ran as UN candidates. And many Créditistes spared no efforts to support the UN campaign, relegating the official Créditiste leader, Camil Samson, and his ultra-right-wing Catholic *Bérêt Blancs* to a folkloric role on the provincial scene. The third political force that the old lion Bellemare dreamed about and Rodrigue Biron put together is to say the least a motley crew. The garious forces are far from being united. Biron will have to do some fancy skating among the various clans that make up what is called the Union Nationale.

The election coffers of the UN were also divided. At the start of the campaign Biron said that the UN had only $100,000. Perhaps he meant that that was the amount he had been told about, because it's an open secret that the UN was once a very wealthy political organization. Maurice Duplessis liked to have his party on a firm financial base — money helps win elections, after all. The UN's old election funds — a good part of which are to be found in numbered Swiss bank accounts — are still maintained by Duplessis' former private secretary, Mademoiselle Bellerose. That lady is responsible for seeing that the money collected by ''le chef'' is still used to carry on the work started by the UN's founder, and so she is very circumspect about how the money is spent. Like Bellemare, she wanted to see Biron before loosening the purse strings too much.

The second stash was kept, in part, by Mario Beaulieu, one of the UN's important backroom boys. This fund was more ''official,'' although there are a number of mysteries surrounding it as well. Beaulieu acted as the party's representative when it sold the newspaper *Montréal-Matin,* and as notary in the sale of the Renaissance Club on Sherbrooke Street in Montreal, one of two such clubs owned by the UN. Several members of the UN are still asking questions about that sale. Beaulieu may have played a role in the company that was formed to acquire the land on which the Place Howard Johnson now stands, the site previously occupied by the Renaissance Club. A coincidence? He even opened a UN office there, and it's said that he's planning to reopen the Renaissance Club on the same site — inside the Howard Johnson complex this time. Biron has had problems with this second coffer too, and party members are asking some serious questions about how the party's funds are being administered — and about who is profiting from them.

The spectacular recovery of the Union Nationale does not necessarily mean a renewal at the grass roots. With respect to women, the attitudes of the UN and of Mr. Biron are pretty much the same as they were during the time of "Quebec's dark ages." Biron doesn't hesitate to say that women's role in the UN — aside from holding coffee parties — is to support their husbands. There wasn't one woman on the UN's strategy committee during the campaign. Women's liberation is most assuredly not one of Biron's concerns. He talks about renewal, but it's hard to find. Is it in the area of party financing? A more democratic internal party structure? The role of women? The policy of addressing voters differently depending on their language or ethnic group?

If the PQ or the Liberals had formed a minority government, Biron would have held the balance of power. A nice role to play, but it didn't work out that way. It will be another four years before Biron will have a chance to prove that the UN's electoral recovery is a long-term phenomenon. He will have to consolidate his position as leader of the party, and cement the fragile unity that exists within it. Most of all, he will have to rid the UN of the people who came close to leading it to the grave. And of course he will have to broaden his electoral base if he doesn't want the UN to be a perpetual third party. Biron wants to take over from the Liberals. To do so, he will have to show the voters that the UN is no longer the "big blue machine," the champion of fear and corruption. The UN will have to learn from its own past mistakes faster than the Liberals do.

In Rodrigue Biron's view, women's role in politics consists of holding coffee parties and supporting their husbands.

4

The Marginal Groups

When the election was called there was a sudden rash of new political parties. It was as though everybody wanted his share, no matter how small, of the pie. New alliances were forged, new parties founded, and for many of those involved it seemed enough to be able to say that they had taken part on November 15.

The Ralliement des Créditistes was, of course, still around. Their share of the popular vote was five per cent, or just under 160,000 votes, as they slid even closer to the bottom than in 1973 when they picked up ten per cent. The Ralliement's recent history has been a stormy one. Their leader, Camil Samson, had the job of gathering together the remnants of his flock that hadn't strayed into the UN fold. Aside from the faithful *Bérêt Blancs*, though, he couldn't point to too many successes. Samson's slogan "One we are and one we stay" is a reflection of the Créditistes' sad fate.

The Créditiste phenomenon is a regional one, concentrated in Abitibi in northwestern Quebec, but even there the PQ wave produced ripples. Luckily Samson was re-elected in his own riding, Rouyn-Noranda, because he must be the most colourful political figure in Quebec. Even ridicule doesn't seem to be able to bring him down. Or the president of his own party, for that matter, who said on the eve of the election: "If the polls show forty-two per cent undecided it means that they're all Créditistes who were given orders not to reveal their true colours if they were asked." The Créditistes are perpetually awaiting the "miracle" to be sent to them by Providence; they enjoy reminiscing about the 1970 upsurge, which saw twelve Créditistes elected, and, even more, about the federal breakthrough in 1962 when the party, under the late Réal Caouette, benefited from strong feelings of discontent and won twenty-six seats. Fervent prayers were addressed to the good Lord in the hope that it would happen again this time.

Samson's campaign was ruined for good on November 7 when he attacked the PQ, which he said was "led by socialists and communists." The PQ was not amused. Samson claimed to have access to a shocking resolution presented to the PQ's national convention that aimed at doing away with elections for a period of ten years. The resolution — still according to Samson — had been narrowly defeated. He went on: "We know what democracy means in socialist countries. You need a passport to go from one city to another." The press, of course, wanted to know where he'd picked up all these "truths"; his reply was: "In a newspaper somewhere." And he added: "You know it as well as I do, it's common knowledge." The PQ, he claimed, had been infiltrated by people "with communistic tendencies and ideologies. . . . When I talk about the PQ it seems that I make the press nervous."

But they mustn't be taken in: the communists had infiltrated "everywhere": the Centrale d'Enseignants du Québec (Quebec Teachers' Central — the union representing the province's French-speaking teachers), Hydro-Quebec and, it goes without

Créditiste leader Camil Samson railed against communist infiltration.

saying, the Church, at least since Vatican II. Following these declarations Samson was asked if he hadn't concluded an agreement with the Liberals, one that, say, would let him hold onto three ridings in the northwestern part of the province if he didn't bother them in east-end Montreal. His reply: "You don't know the Créditistes very well if you think we can be bribed like that."

The Parti National Populaire (PNP), founded in 1975 by former Liberal Justice Minister Jérôme Choquette, made a pitiful showing, getting barely one per cent of the vote in the thirty-six ridings where it ran candidates. Choquette lost his own seat in Outremont, coming a poor third behind the Liberal and PQ candidates. Only Fabien Roy won his seat in the rural riding of Beauce-sud where he got 27,000 votes. There's no doubt that the voters of Beauce-sud voted not for the party but for their man. Choquette, whose image was always that of a man of integrity, albeit right-wing, ran a highly unoriginal campaign. It lacked colour and imagination and compared with Samson's, it was a deadly bore.

It's hard to imagine what sort of future there might be for the PNP, although Choquette keeps insisting that the recent election was only "a dress rehearsal," since they were without a serious platform, organization and, most important, money. Even though the PNP used the campaign as "a first step, a springboard for the next provincial election," it's obvious that neither Choquette nor Fabien Roy has any political future outside the UN, which they tried unsuccessfully to join, or the Liberal party. Choquette made only one interesting statement during the campaign: "If the government was so weak in administration it's because it's too closely associated with big money interests. It can't simply cut the ties that bind it to the people who keep the coffers filled."

The most original of the new political parties was the Democratic Alliance (DA). Led by two Montreal city councillors from the opposition Montreal Citizens Movement (MCM), Nick Auf der Maur and Bob Keaton, the DA ran candidates in thirteen Montreal ridings where there is a large proportion of English-speaking voters. The DA professed to be a consolidation of "moderate progressives," rather like the MCM on the municipal scene, that would allow English-speaking voters to free themselves from their role as "hostages" (to use Lévesque's word) of the Liberals. It was, of course, accused of being a Péquiste fifth column in the English-speaking community, and that may not be totally false, because the DA's candidates seemed to be rather sympathetic to the PQ, although in disagreement with its stand on the language question.

The DA got just under 15,000 votes, and ran good campaigns

The PNP campaign, led by Jérôme Choquette (third from left) never caught on.

in Westmount, where Auf der Maur was the candidate, and Nôtre-Dame-de-Grâce, where Keaton lost to Bryce Mackasey. It had been put together a little too quickly and would likely have done much better if the candidates had been able to present a more "provincial" vision, or at least a broader one. Its platform was based too exclusively on municipal questions. Still, it would have been interesting to have at least one DA member in the National Assembly; sympathetic to the PQ, he or she might have been named the only "anglophone" cabinet minister.

Then there was the NDP-Québec, led by Henri-François Gautrin. It took one more step towards becoming a marginal force; it virtually went underground, having joined forces with a left-wing union faction called the Regroupement des Militants Syndicaux (Grouping of Union Militants). Altogether, they brought in fewer than 2500 votes. It was said that their combined forces represented the beginning of a "real" workers' party, but it got off to a very inauspicious start. As for Moscow's agents in Quebec, the Communist Party of Quebec, observers are still wondering just how its "secretary-general" managed to get thirty votes in the very "proletarian" riding of Maisonneuve. Even the Parti des Travailleurs du Québec (Quebec Workers' Party) did better — without Brezhnev!

5

Bill 22: Bourassa's Achilles Heel

Never before in a Quebec provincial election had New Canadian voters — particularly the Italians — been courted so assiduously. In the past, Montreal's 200,000 Italians had faithfully voted Liberal. It was the party that offered them the best guarantee of social advancement within Canada. Italians in the Montreal suburb of St-Léonard had been involved in a language controversy in September 1969, but it was the promulgation of Bill 22, in July 1974, that placed the Italian community at the centre of the language of education debate, one that is crucial to the future of Quebec.

The Bourassa government, seeking a compromise that would please everybody, instead pulled off the *tour de force* of leaving everybody unhappy. Attempts to limit access to English schools by testing prospective pupils' knowledge of English were widely resented in the Italian community as discriminatory and harmful to the morale of five- and six-year-old children. Since the measures did not apply to the English community, the Italians felt that they had been relegated to the role of second-class citizens.

Thus the burden of government policy in this area fell the hardest on a community that was actually very close to French-speaking Quebecers.

The Italians had generally been wise enough not to fall into the trap set for them by some of the harder-line English on the West Island. The English felt threatened in the long term because of their minority position in Quebec, and feared losing the privileges conferred on them by virtue of their majority status within Canada as a whole. In certain English-speaking circles, attempts were made to associate the Italians with the safeguarding of these privileges.

The Italian community was offered two vastly different courses of action for coping with Bill 22. The first was proposed by the Italian-Canadian Federation, a highly traditional organization. Its president, Giuseppe di Battista, provided a good summary of its thinking when he said: "The Federation didn't want to take part in the demonstrations against Bill 22. We preferred to use other means of persuasion and to establish a dialogue with the authorities." It's not surprising that many Italians did not go along with this wait-and-see strategy, dependent as it was on the good will of the Department of Education.

The more dynamic elements in the community opted for more effective means to obtain justice, at the very moment when signs and rumours suggested that a new law would be presented in the National Assembly. In 1973 these people, who represented a new kind of leadership in the Italian community, formed the Consiglio Educativo Italo-Canadese. Unlike the old Federation, the Consiglio promised to mobilize the Italian community. It was behind the demonstrations, petitions, occupations of schools and parallel English classes. But despite all this action, Bourassa turned a deaf ear.

The Consiglio consists of only six members: three school principals, a priest in the Italian parish of Notre-Dame de Pompéï; a school administrator, Donato Taddeo; and a CEGEP (junior college) teacher, Angelo Montini, who is the Consiglio's

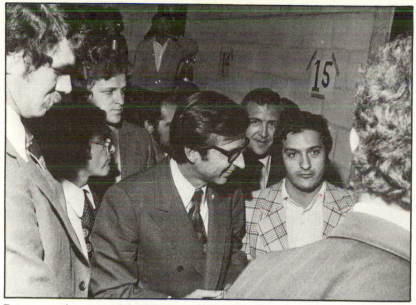
Bourassa tries to explain Bill 22 to Italian parents.

president. Because of the importance of the language question in the 1976 election campaign, I spoke to Montini to find out more about the Consiglio's policies. He told me several days before the election:

> We don't want Bill 22 abolished, we just want article 5 [establishing the language tests] erased. The Consiglio's main strength comes from the fact that we recognize that Quebec is French-speaking. We agree that the French language must be protected. We don't dispute the sections of the Bill that deal with billboards and the language of work. What we're opposed to is discrimination in the language of education through the adoption of provisions that put us in an unfair position relative to English-speaking parents. We didn't want to incite violence between the Italians and French-speaking Quebecers, we wanted to channel the feelings of our community, to control them and avoid excessive hostility.

It was particularly important for us not to be identified with the English-speaking community; what we did was decide to concentrate our efforts where they were most needed, on the schools. We told the Italian community: You want English schools because you know English? All right, the Bill allows that. Besides, to cite just one case, that of the Jérôme-LeRoyer School Commission [in St-Léonard], it couldn't provide English-language kindergarten classes, even though [the less restrictive] Bill 63 was in effect, and now Bill 22 has given our demands short shrift, despite all the solemn promises.

But Montini's mind was less on the struggles of the past two years than on the election campaign then underway in which, as he explained, the Italian community was being shaken by a strong current of frustration:

Basically, we were screwed by the Government. They expected the Italians to go on voting Liberal the way they've always done. They liked to think we had no other choice. But the Consiglio told our people: "You're completely out of it; you're going to stick with the Liberals but they aren't going to change a thing." That's how we politicized them, by explaining to them just what we were going to do. We told them that as far as the political parties were concerned we were neutral. We didn't want to burn out too soon. And they followed us. The proof is that they turned out to our meetings in large numbers. And besides they forced themselves to keep their tempers under control.

Paradoxically, though, Donato Taddeo, one of the leaders of the Consiglio, ran for the Liberals in the Montreal working-class riding of St-Henri. Montini explained:

A month before the election was called the Liberals came and asked Mr. Taddeo and me if we'd run for them. They wanted to shut us up, you see! Mr. Taddeo accepted. They didn't make any secret arrangements with him, though they let him know that the law would be amended to allow for freedom of choice. They did add, however, that it couldn't be done during the campaign. Mr. Taddeo believed them, but he added that if nothing had changed between now and next March he'd pull out. I was suspicious of their promises, but he wasn't, so I can understand why he ran. The Italians in St-Henri were very critical of Taddeo for running. He's still a member of the Consiglio but he wasn't consulted about strategy during the campaign.

The Consiglio was obviously the victim of pressure from the *rouge* machine, because it was said that its anti-government position would help the PQ win some of the east-end Montreal ridings. "Of course there were pressures on us," Montini said. "There were even death threats — about fifteen against me and the parish priest. Kidnapping threats too." Where did these threats come from? He hesitated for a moment, then replied:

> Let's say they probably came from the Liberal machine. People came to make trouble at our meetings too — in Bourassa riding [formerly held by Lise Bacon] they said it was people from the Liberal machine. Maybe there were some Mafia types connected with the machine too. Just take a look at the anti-Consiglio propaganda in the newspaper *Il Corriere,* which is controlled by the Liberals. I don't want to get on the wrong side of anybody, but they control the Italian television too, and they used it to denigrate us.

Montini did not wish to identify further these infiltrators, but I was told by reliable sources that "it's Cornelli's gang, who are close to Cagliari and Cotroni [identified as Montreal Mafia chieftains]."

The election campaign allowed the Consiglio to step up its demands, putting the government against the wall. It didn't miss a chance, and pressed its demands with considerable tactical skill. It called a meeting of all Italian parents and invited the political parties to come and explain their positions on the sub-

Bill 22: Bourassa's Achilles Heel 77

ject. Thus the Consiglio challenged the government to bring in modifications — otherwise it would risk losing votes, and more particularly, certain key ridings in Montreal. On October 23, Bourassa, speaking in the riding of Johnson, had reaffirmed his intention not to modify Bill 22 during the election campaign; but he made an about-face on November 2, just a few days before the Consiglio's meeting. Bourassa's improvised solution consisted in essence of shelving the language tests for children who already had members of their family in English schools. In the same vein, he announced that changes would be brought about so that English would be taught in French schools beginning in the third grade. This promise, made under pressure, didn't appease the Consiglio, which wasted no time in denouncing it, emphasizing that the changes were only superficial.

The stage was set, then, for a rally held on Sunday, November 7, at the Notre-Dame de Pompéï church. By two in the afternoon 2000 people were crowded into the church basement. The atmosphere was decidedly overheated. Understandably, neither Bourassa nor his Education Minister, Jean Bienvenue, wanted to be abused by the crowd, and it was left to Solicitor-General Fernand Lalonde to serve as the target for the crowd's anger at the government. The PQ representative clearly and calmly restated his party's program; the crowd appreciated his frankness and received him politely. Biron, on the other hand, with his policy of a return to freedom of choice in the Bill 63 style, won the favour of the dissatisfied audience.

Following the meeting, something had changed in the political life of the Italian community, as Montini explained:

> The Italians are still Liberals, even though they're going to vote UN this time. The Consiglio didn't send out a specific message to vote UN, but we pushed them so that that's the only conclusion they could draw. The Italian vote will be a vote of

non-confidence in the government. It isn't a vote against the Liberals: the Italians are going to vote against Bourassa.

After the election Montini confirmed that the Italians had, in fact, voted *en masse* — more than sixty per cent — against the Bourassa government. He also spoke of the Italian community's feeling of apprehension with respect to the new government:

> The Italians are apprehensive, but they aren't about to panic. For them the PQ is reminiscent of a kind of autocracy that they knew in Europe: fascism and so forth. In the past, certain Péquistes defended an excessive kind of nationalism. When these people heard about the PQ they thought of war, the FLQ. Although the PQ's a left-wing party the factions inside it range from far right to far left, so it isn't all that clear. Certain progressive Italians like the social democratic part of their platform, but they're still federalists. They'll vote against independence.

The new government will have to lend an attentive ear to these New Canadians — or New Québécois. Here is what the Consiglio intends to propose to the new Minister of Education:

Possible Solutions

Short Term

1) Integrate children into the English sector on a rough quota basis rather than following a standardized procedure. Automatically accept all those children who already have a brother or sister in the English school system. Accept those children who scored more than sixty per cent in the comprehension part of the language test but failed the expression part. (We believe that this discrepancy has more to do with the constraints of the tests or other psychological problems than lack of knowledge of the language, since they have demonstrated an ability to understand it.)

2) For children who fail the tests and are obliged to attend French schools, offer pilot courses in which both French and English are taught beginning in the first year.

Long Term

For ALL landed immigrants who choose to live in Quebec and who arrive in Quebec after the eventual new regulations concerning the application of article 5 of Bill 22 have been put into effect, obligatory French immersion in kindergarten and elementary school. Language of instruction could be made a matter of choice beginning at the secondary rather than at the CEGEP level.

N.B. This would not apply to those who are already here, nor to their children's children, nor would it apply retroactively.

ADVANTAGES of such a solution:

a) Elimination of the need for language tests.

b) The survival of the English sector would be no more threatened than it is now.

c) Only real immigrants, and ALL of them, would be affected by such regulations.

d) French-speaking citizens and Bill 22 would be protected.

N.B. Such a solution would have to take account of people who might stay in Quebec only temporarily. The following amendment could apply in these cases: "For those who are not landed immigrants and whose mother tongue is not English — obligatory French schooling."

The Italian press did not follow the same line during the election campaign as the Consiglio. The largest Italian weekly in Montreal, *Il Corriere*, well known for its support of the Liberal party, waged a campaign against the Consiglio. It questioned their true motives: *"Consiglio educativo o Comizio electorale?"* The paper commented on the rally at Notre-Dame de Pompéï: "We want to point out . . . the futility, the uselessness for the Italian cause, the demagoguery of such a rally, the fruit of a skilful organization working in support of a certain party. When Montini reiterated his claim that 'We're not engaged in politics here,' he sounded too much like a new Ulysses, listening to the song of the sirens."

Il Corriere went on to point out that the meeting had been a trap set for Fernand Lalonde, and that its goal had been to give support to Biron's party. The reporter rejected the solutions of the PQ and the UN, dismissing them as "utopian and futuristic," and called on the Liberals' supporters to be unanimous and strong; in that way, he concluded, the future of the Italians would be assured in the province. *Il Corriere's* faith in the Liberal party went so far that it crowned Lise Bacon, the MNA for Bourassa, a riding in which twenty-six per cent of the voters are Italian, "*Notre-Dame degli Italiani.*" (This didn't prevent Bacon from losing her seat, however.)

Another weekly, *Tribuna Italiana,* to everyone's surprise, gave its support to the PQ, finding that the Liberal government had been discredited and that "Bourassa's companions are dramatically incapable of transformation . . . The Liberals are reduced to begging for votes and confidence in the most pitiful way. The only party that has spoken to New Quebecers clearly on the problem of the language of education — and with a clarity that was rather 'tough' — is the PQ. That's what we really need." For this paper the PQ was a left-wing party with a social democratic platform; it was reassured by the guarantee of a referendum, but was opposed to independence. Only the weekly *Cittadino Canadese* took the same position as the Consiglio, rejecting the line that a vote for the UN was a vote for the separatists.

6

Labour and the campaign

In 1972, when Marcel Pepin, then president of the Confederation of National Trade Unions (CNTU), was released from Orsainville prison, where he had been held with the two other major Quebec union leaders, his message was "Bring down the Liberal régime!" The Bourassa government had passed an emergency law forcing striking civil servants back to work. The three union leaders had been jailed for inciting their members to disobey the law.

The 1972 strike marked the culmination of a six-year-long confrontation between the Quebec government and the unions. During those six years the province had the worst social climate it has ever experienced. Quebec's record of strikes in every area of its economy — asbestos, mining and smelting, construction, airplane parts, the automobile industry, police, firemen, transportation workers, teachers and the health professions — was second only to Italy's. Few sectors escaped this deterioration in labour-management relations.

Bourassa set the tone by allowing conflicts in the public and para-public sector to worsen. He was accused of being too soft by some, too tough by others; he never found the happy medium.

The Quebec employers' group, the Conseil du Patronat, blamed him for unwarranted meddling in their affairs while the unions accused him of repressive tactics directed against workers.

Of all groups, the unions were probably the most dissatisfied with the Bourassa régime. The government has passed no fewer that five special laws since 1973: in 1974, it was a law giving the government full powers over the construction industry; in 1975, a law putting an end to a strike at the Montreal Urban Community Transit Commission; in 1976, one law forced striking teachers to return to their classrooms, another aimed at maintaing essential services in hospitals while yet another put an end to a nurses' strike. Union leaders were quick to say that the Bourassa government was the champion of special laws. The events of 1976 in the public sector certainly bore them out.

But Bourassa had also failed to deal with problems considered essential by the unions: unemployment, housing, the health and safety of workers, the role of women in the labour force, the inaccessibility of unions to a large segment of the labour force. The unions resented large companies' hard line in labour conflicts and what they regarded as their increasingly violent exploitation of Quebec workers. The Liberal régime had done nothing concrete to resolve these problems.

Jean Cournoyer had promised a law on industrial accidents when he was Labour Minister, but it never came about; the law to compensate victims of asbestosis lacked teeth; and the fate of the Beaudry report on the deplorable situation in the asbestos mines is still unknown. The last Minister of Labour, Gérald Harvey, promised legislation to reform the labour code and to raise the minimum wage, but nothing was done. In the construction industry, after the Cliche Commission had handed in its report the government saw fit to enact only some of the recommendations — those that were aimed at cracking down on the unions.

Bourassa appears unperturbed as he is heckled by striking Alcan workers.

Unionized workers weren't too crazy about Bourassa.

Then along came his election campaign, with one of its themes being to "bring down" the unions. Bourassa's pre-taped message gave this explanation:

> We must re-examine the balance among the various social groups in our community. We believe that union freedom is legitimate and compatible with the social and economic progress that are our priorities. But it has become obvious that some labour leaders no longer respect the social contract established in 1964. There have been unacceptable abuses of the right to strike, abuses that at times have represented acts of cruelty directed at innocent and deprived people. Present conditions must be changed and we're going to do just that.

Borrowing an idea from Gaullist France, Bourassa proposed the abolition of the right to strike in hospitals with a plan to bring in legislation that would allow the government to force employees back to work by "requisition" without National Assembly approval. During the campaign Bourassa even spoke about controlling union finances so that "dues would really be used to serve the workers' interests."

As a result of all this, the unions campaigned against the government. The most active and open battle was waged by the Quebec Federation of Labour (QFL), the largest central with its 272,000 members. As expected, the QFL backed the PQ, but it was not unconditional support. For example, President Louis Laberge said that he still did not agree with the PQ's stance favouring independence. He added, though, that Lévesque's party was the only one that offered workers the possibility of defending their position, thanks to its democractic structures, no counterpart of which existed in the other parties.

The CNTU and the CEQ (Quebec Teachers' Central) on the other hand didn't come out in favour of any party, stating that none of them really represented the interests of the workers. The CNTU, ardently hoping for a Liberal defeat, was sly in the way it did its work. During the campaign it kept repeating that Bourassa and the Liberals had to be beaten to teach this most anti-union of governments a lesson, but it was careful to add that the PQ was "at the service of the dominant, exploiting class." CNTU President Norbert Rodrigue even pointed out that "the PQ doesn't reject capitalism." The CNTU's position, then, was a rather passive one, and the CEQ's was virtually the same.

The CEQ, though, did publish a report on the disastrous state of public finances under the Bourassa government. The report explained that Quebec's public finances verged on the catastrophic. Every dollar of tax revenue was mortgaged to the extent of thirty-six cents through government borrowing. Under the Liberals, Quebec's borrowing had shot up from $550 million to $3.3 billion, an increase of 500 per cent, while during the same period tax revenue had increased by only 154 per cent. The CEQ also dealt with the decline in social services, education and health care, areas where spending had been curbed in favour of helping private enterprise. It predicted that the policy of freezing these services would be followed by one that would reduce them. The document gave several examples of measures directed toward helping private enterprise, such as the construction at a cost of $25 million by the government forestry corporation, Rexfor, of a sawmill on the Outardes river on the north shore of the St. Lawrence. This sawmill would go to a private company, Quebec North Shore.

It wasn't surprising, then, that the union leaders claimed victory on November 15. For them, the Liberal defeat was even more important than the PQ victory. They had rid themselves of their worst enemy. Although Bourassa had never been able to get his campaign messages across, including the one on labour relations, the unions saw his defeat as a defeat for the anti-union forces. They felt that for the first time in years the government would be reasonably sympathetic to workers' demands.

Louis Laberge put it this way: ''We've never concealed the fact that there are differences of opinion between the PQ and the union movement on certain points, but we think we'll be able now to talk freely and openly with the new government about the workers' demands.'' The labour leaders held the Liberal government fully responsible for the unhealthy social climate that had prevailed in Quebec since 1970. They hoped the PQ victory would mean that the new government would respect the rights of wage-earners rather than trying to trample them. There was even talk that ''a new social contract'' might be established.

The PQ has often been accused of being too closely tied to the unions. It's true that some of the new government MNAs have come from the union movement: Robert Burns, Guy Chevrette and Guy Bisaillon, for example. But these men did not come to the PQ as representatives of their unions. They came as individuals. The PQ is essentially a reformist, nationalist party. Although it has a social democratic program, the PQ is not a social democratic party in the same sense as the New Democratic Party in Canada, Sweden's Social Democratic Party or the British Labour Party, all of which have organic links to the labour movement.

This kind of political association is foreign to the PQ. Take the case of Rodrigue Tremblay: it's hard to imagine that he was speaking for the CEQ or the CNTU when he announced his delight at the fall of the Allende government in Chile and the death of its leader. Membership in the PQ has always been based on its political program rather than on an individual's class origins. René Lévesque, Jacques Parizeau and Guy Joron, to mention only three, have never been part of the union movement;

in fact they have often been on the other side of the fence. The secretary general of the CNTU, Jean Thibault, does not hesitate to say about Jacques Parizeau: "He's the one that gave us a boot in the arse with his wage policies in the days of Lesage."

Although the QFL was the only union group that supported the PQ during the campaign, its president readily admitted: "We don't owe the PQ anything and they don't owe us anything." Shortly after the election, Lévesque spoke on this subject during an appearance on the CBC-TV public affairs program *le 60,* saying: "Sure we're prejudiced in favour of the workers; they make up the majority of our population. But our government isn't going to have its hands tied by the unions or by high finance or low finance either." CNTU president Norbert Rodrigue went even further: "The PQ victory represented a victory for the people, the ordinary guy, and the CNTU figures we won this election because we got rid of Bourassa; but still it's the union movement, not the PQ, that speaks for organized labour in Quebec, and the CNTU hasn't dropped the idea of working to create a real workers' party."

On the whole, the union movement has for a long time been far ahead of the PQ on the question of the social future of Quebec. While the PQ talked about building a more humane and civilized society within the capitalist system, militant unionists talked about abolishing the same system and replacing it with a re-volutionary form of socialism. The only union that has une-quivocally supported the PQ in recent years is the United Steel-workers (QFL). Its president, Jean Gérin-Lajoie, explains:

> What I object to is the creation of a class-based party for a class struggle, a class-based power. I think that democratic parliamen-tary values are part of left-wing values. We want action toward social democracy. The PQ's program satisfies our members' social aspirations and requirements, there's no doubt about that.

The vote shows it. We aren't trying to push the PQ further to the left; what we want to do is try to win everybody over to their present program. I haven't the slightest desire to make the PQ program more radical when it's obvious that they still haven't convinced the majority. People who say that the ideology of a workers' party is incompatible with the PQ's ideology are absolutely right. Class analysis has nothing to do with social reality; that kind of concept comes out of books, not real life. It's an analytical tool that has no value when it comes to action.

Needless to say, a number of militant unionists consider Gérin-Lajoie to be counter-revolutionary and even anti-union. Still, his position is a perfect capsule of the point of view of the so-called left-wing Péquistes. There is a considerable distance between this left wing and the left wing of the union movement. The Steelworkers were the only union that gave the PQ concrete support during the campaign, particularly in their stronghold, Sept-Iles, in the riding of Duplessis.

The PQ offers the unions a new approach to labour relations. It is reasonable to expect that the PQ will try to avoid Bourassa-style confrontations and that consequently the social climate in Quebec will be better in years to come. And while the union leaders will continue to press for their "essential" demands, the ordinary members, the vast majority of whom voted for the PQ, will exert pressure on their leaders to come to terms with the new government. This last element should not be underestimated, because the rank and file has a voice within the unions.

One thing that should not be expected is the kind of flirtation that went on in 1960 between Jean Marchand and the CNTU on the one hand and the Lesage government on the other. Norbert Rodrigue is clear on this point: "Bourassa's collapse was a great relief but we can't afford to repeat the illusions of 1960." On the eve of the Quiet Revolution the unions expected to become equal partners with the employers and the state. The honeymoon lasted a few years, during which the union movement made important advances in the public sector, with public employees attaining the right to strike. With the hospital strike in 1966 and the Montreal public transit strike in 1967, a new chapter of confrontations between the unions and the state began, and illusions on both sides were put to an end.

While in the early sixties international and provincial circumstances assured increasing economic prosperity, the capitalist countries of the West are currently undergoing their worst economic and monetary crisis since the thirties. Despite the good will of the parties involved, external conditions are such that social conflicts can only be exacerbated. No one should be surprised, then, if Quebec's domestic squabbling gets worse in the next few months or years.

For some years now the union movement has been trying unsuccessfully to persuade successive governments to bring in legislation that would allow the vast majority of workers access to union membership. This is particularly important since barely thirty-three per cent of the labour force in Quebec is currently unionized, even when company unions are included. Although this demand may be justified it's important to know who stands to benefit from it. The workers do, of course, but also — and most important — it would serve to increase the social and political power of union bureaucrats. If the union leaders could enlarge their social base — a necessary prior condition for forming a true social democratic party — they then might be able to envisage moving on to challenge the PQ in the political arena.

7

Wait and See: Business and the election

"A Parti Québécois victory would be hell. They're a bunch of bastards who are out to destroy us." That was whiskey king Charles Bronfman's comment on the eve of the election to a select audience from the Montreal Jewish community, and it didn't go unnoticed. It was published the next day in the Montreal *Star*, just in time to be read by English-speaking voters on their way to the polls. Bronfman even threatened to pack his bags and move to Ontario, taking his baseball team, the Montreal Expos, with him. His remarks might have induced a measure of panic but they certainly didn't make much sense in a business context, for what Bronfman feared did come about, and there could be a danger that his comments might have repercussions for the Seagram company of which he is president.

It's hard to understand Bronfman's fear about the survival of the Jewish community under a Péquiste régime, the prospect of which seemed to remind him of the Arabs. Bronfman is intelligent and it's surprising he would risk possible financial losses with his remarks. Or was there something more to the story? Could this have been a way to persuade the English-speaking electorate not to vote Union Nationale and let separatism in by the back door? Whatever the answer, Bronfman is now in the position of having to deal with the people he described as "bastards."

Bronfman wasn't the only one to put in his two cents' worth. Elsewhere in the business community, however, the watchword was obviously prudence. This probably corresponded to a need to reassure shareholders and avoid any unfavourable developments on the stock exchange. Several statements are worthy of note. Kenneth White, president of Royal Trust, issued a cautious statement that contrasted with the Liberals' propaganda: he said that he wasn't afraid of the PQ's coming to power. Royal Trust has assets of $3 billion in Quebec, and is an influential and well-connected corporation. A vice-president of the Royal Bank, commenting on the transfer of large sums of money out of Quebec after the publication of the poll that gave the PQ the lead, remarked: "Such actions are irrational and useless, because we're subject to federal laws." After the drop of the Canadian dollar on the foreign exchange market, which Bourassa made such a fuss about, the widely respected Conference Board of Canada pointed out that the election had very little to do with this drop.

The PQ seemed to make a better impression in business circles than it had in the past. When Lévesque spoke on radio station CFCF he emphasized the lack of influence that radical elements had inside the party. And he was listened to attentively by the Canadian Club, meeting-place of the financial establishment in Montreal.

A few days before the election was called, the PQ leader spoke to the Chamber of Commerce in Ste-Foy, summarizing his economic policies. He said:

> Our basic option is to favour those instruments that we control (co-operatives, the state, Quebec capital). That way we hope to be able to put our priorities in order by giving foreign investments

Quebec's new finance minister, Jacques Parizeau.

only the secondary role that they should play in a self-respecting society . . . It's obvious that we can't stake our development solely on a traditional capitalist model, so we must work with state institutions and the co-operative movement.

Some members of the business community expressed a measure of confidence in the PQ during the election campaign. Among those were the president of St. Lawrence Colombium, which was faced with competition from a multinational, and the Conseil des Hommes d'Affaires Québécois (Quebec Businessmen's Council), whose position was stated in these terms: "The sovereignty of Quebec could only help businessmen and enable the majority of Quebec firms to expand."

The president of the Canadian Manufacturers Association, Rodrigue Bilodeau, took a different stand, however. He predicted that "the separation of Quebec would oust Canadian manufacturers from the Quebec market in favour of foreign interests." He added that "there would be a major fragmentation of our market . . . Canadian manufacturers who have trouble competing would have to give in to foreign competition . . . A large number of Canadians across the country would see their jobs threatened."

These two opposed positions are significant. What they mean is that a choice between federalism and sovereignty is not simply a personal choice; rather, it has to do with who will control the Quebec market.

The Mouvement Desjardins is one financial organization that would benefit from independence. Its president, Joseph Rouleau, although he was careful not to appear partisan, seems to have understood this. This at any rate is one possible interpretation of remarks he made to the Montreal Chamber of Commerce on November 2: "If the federal government persists in refusing to give Quebec adequate political power and fiscal means to ensure its economic and cultural survival, Quebecers will have to ask some careful questions about their present condition and their future within Confederation.''

And on November 15 when the results were in, the sky didn't fall. Foreign investors, notably those who loan money to Quebec, seemed surprised at first, but less so than might have been expected. Aside from Charles Bronfman's threats, there doesn't appear to have been any massive flight of capital. In large New York brokerage houses René Lévesque's article ''For an independent Quebec'', published in the July 1976 issue of *Foreign Affairs* (and reproduced as an appendix to this book), was being carefully reread. In the next few months these people would be listening carefully to Quebec, and studying their files. Their attitude was the typically American one: Wait and see.

8

The Hidden Stakes of November 15

The outcome of the November 15 election can be analysed in a number of ways. It might be considered to be an outright rejection of Prime Minister Trudeau, as it is obvious that federal government policies had a considerable bearing on the results of the election. In that light, a look at the relationship between the federal government and the provinces — particularly Quebec — in the past decade might be instructive.

We must go back to the time when Lester Pearson was Prime Minister, when he was accused of softness toward the U.S. in such areas as the auto pact and the placement of nuclear missile bases on Canadian soil (to which his predecessor, John Diefenbaker, had been fiercely opposed). In this era, Finance Minister Walter Gordon's measures aimed at gaining the Canadian economy back from American investors met a sad fate.

Pearson was also soft with respect to Quebec, in the area of the transfer of taxation powers and also on the question of family allowances, a controversy in which Lévesque was Quebec's champion. The arrival of the ''three wise men'' (Trudeau, Marchand and Pelletier) in Ottawa in 1965 was the first step toward a change in the relationship. Trudeau's dazzling ascent to the highest political office in the country — helped by the complicity of most of the news media in creating Trudeaumania — ushered in a period of rigidity toward the provinces and tense relations with the U.S. The two components of this phenomenon, which is still not entirely understood, were on the one hand Ottawa's new foreign policy and on the other the strongest centralizing tendency ever seen in Canada.

When transcripts of the Nixon tapes were published during the Watergate scandal it was amusing to note the former President's lack of respect for his Canadian counterpart. Nixon's comments about Trudeau reflected the tensions that existed between the two countries. U.S. ambassadors to Canada were given the task of bringing these frictions into the open. A few examples in the area of the economy may be mentioned: the lowering of the import quota on American beef and the export quota on oil and natural gas; the law governing foreign investments; the abolition of tax deductions for Canadian advertisers in *Time* and *Readers' Digest* and on American TV stations located near the Canadian border.

Trudeau was also responsible for innovations in Canadian foreign policy that might be described as slaps in the face to the policies of Henry Kissinger. Canada went all out to establish a "contractual link" with the European Common Market, which was the touchstone of its new orientation; Trudeau's 1976 trip to Japan had similar aims. He made a number of moves that were guaranteed to displease Washington — notably Canada's recognition of Mao's China and rupture with Taiwan in 1970. Trudeau's trip to Latin America took him to Mexico (where President Echeverria had become a spokesman for a new international economic order), to Venezuela (a member of the Organization of Petroleum Exporting Countries, Kissinger's "nightmare") and finally, to Cuba, where he received one of the warmest receptions ever given a western head of government. There probably wasn't much rejoicing in the White House at Trudeau's "Viva Castro! Viva Cuba!" and Fidel's reply of "Viva Trudeau! Viva Canada!"

The culmination of all this occurred in July 1976, when Trudeau refused to allow the Taiwanese delegation to participate in the Olympics under the name of the Republic of China. Canada's international role under Trudeau has attracted much attention. There was, for example, our participation in world monetary reform; the inevitability of inviting Canada to partici- pate in the summit of the leading western countries in Puerto Rico; Canada's co-chairmanship with Venezuela of the North- South Dialogue in Paris; Canadian leadership at the conferences on the law of the sea, where it has insisted on significant exten- sions of the rights of coastal states.

The election gave Pierre Trudeau much to think about.

The international balance sheet was an impressive one, then, while at home there was a state of confusion. The contrast is striking. But as we will see later, there was a close relationship between Canada's diplomatic successes abroad and the activities at home of the man who had come to power amid the widespread expectation that he would "put Quebec in its place." Quebec is the most demanding of the provinces. From his first term in office, Trudeau worked at concentrating power and prerogatives in the hands of the central government. There was, for example, Ottawa's refusal to accede to the demands of the provinces concerning taxes and its intervention — not provided for in the Constitution — in municipal affairs through the Ministry of State for Urban Affairs. The federal government expanded its role in another primarily provincial area, that of labour legislation. It also lost no time in taking over in areas that could not have been foreseen in a hundred-year-old constitution, such as recreation, consumer protection, communications and the protection of the environment.

Three important dates show that Trudeau's régime has been the most centralizing one since Confederation, going beyond even Mackenzie King's:

> ● Following the Yom Kippur War in 1973, the oil-exporting countries increased the price of crude oil considerably. This provoked a panic, no doubt exaggerated, that was used to justify federal intervention in an area that had been jealously guarded by the provinces: energy resources. Ottawa took advantage of the occasion to play a leading role in setting prices for the national market.

> ● In October 1975, when the international economic crisis was building, Trudeau imposed controls on prices, wages and profits. He presented the provinces with a *fait accompli;* all that was left

for them to do was to look after the areas that fell under their jurisdiction.

● In March 1976, the Prime Minister threatened to pull off a coup against the provinces by unilaterally repatriating the Constitution from London without previously seeking the agreement of the provinces.

This record suggests an obvious desire to submit the provinces to the "diktat" of federal power. The best example of this is the way in which Trudeau publicly insulted the Premier of Quebec, on the thorny question of the repatriation of the Constitution, in March 1976. He stated his intentions as follows:

What it means is that we want to take away from England — a foreign country, but a friendly one — the right to make laws for Canadians. It shouldn't be too hard to come to an agreement on that . . . So what we're saying is this: let's agree to repatriate the Constitution, let's do it without any talk about the division of powers, our squabbles can wait till later, we don't need the Queen for a referee . . . If we don't agree, we don't agree; if we do agree, then we agree. We won't need the Pope either. We can do it all by ourselves . . . Maybe at some point we might even wonder if we could do it all by ourselves [without the provinces] . . . if it isn't just a simple matter of the Canadian parliament going and saying to England, okay, stop making our laws for us.

No prime minister has ever had the gall to tamper in such a way with provincial rights. The provinces unanimously rejected the threat of a constitutional *coup d'état*. Public opinion and the press rejected it as well, particularly in Quebec. (But why was Bourassa unable to be more firm in the face of such a threat?) At a provincial premiers' meeting in Toronto in the fall of 1976, Premier Lougheed of Alberta, speaking for his colleagues, said the following: "As I've already mentioned with respect to repatriation, the provinces have expressed the opinion that if repatriation is desirable it should nevertheless be accompanied by broadened provincial jurisdiction and authority in certain areas." Since then, and particularly since November 15, 1976, Trudeau has been more cautious.

The domestic and international processes may seem unrelated, and composed of isolated events. While there are no doubt several possible explanations of the policies of the federal Liberals during Trudeau's prime ministership, the following one may shed some new light on the matter.

It may be a commonplace to say that political power is related to economic interests, but this statement may help in understanding the forces in whose name Trudeau and his government are acting. Despite foreign control of many sectors of the economy, there are some gigantic industrial, commercial and financial enterprises controlled by Canadians — for example, Bell Canada, Northern Telecom, Canadian Pacific, Power Corporation, Argus Corporation, Home Oil, Alcan, Brascan, Noranda Mines, Imasco, Stelco, Dofasco, Dominion Textiles and all the Canadian banks. All these economic interests also have foreign holdings, and some of them are among the largest Canadian exporters.

The international economic crisis that has been so acute since 1973 affects not only individuals but large Canadian corporations as well. Wage increases obtained by the unions, the high rate of inflation, falling productivity and rates of profit have not only reduced the competitiveness of Canadian exports but have obliged Ottawa to intervene drastically in the marketplace in order to create a more stable environment for the corporations. This was behind the most draconian economic measures undertaken since World War II. Concentration of planning power and of economic control is essential to the well-being of these interests. To find themselves restrained by several provincial juris-

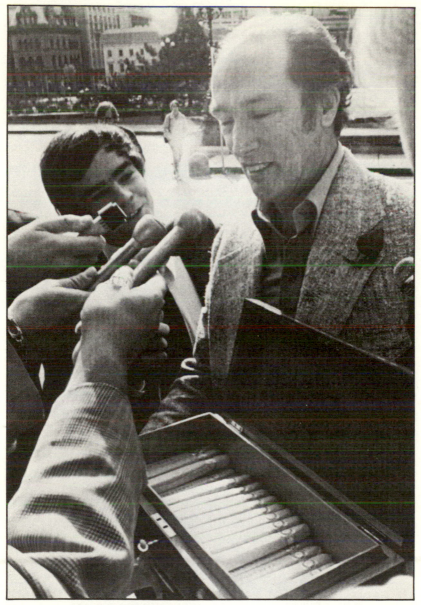

Trudeau in happier times: the outcome of the election represented a serious challenge to his form of federalism.

dictions in such vital matters would be a great disadvantage to them.

Among the provinces, Ontario benefits most from this centralization, both because of its geographical location and because of its level of technological advancement. In the past, Alberta and Quebec have picked up most of the spillover that Ontario couldn't use. In the case of oil-rich Alberta, large interests such as Imperial Oil, Home Oil and the like found Ottawa's energy measures inhibiting. Perhaps some powerful elements in the province had hoped to have free access to the American market.

In the case of Quebec, the situation is more complex. Montreal is the base for a number of multinationals and other giant companies, but they can be excluded at the outset, for they operate essentially in the context of the Canadian and international markets, and are on the whole only incidentally part of the Quebec economy. Apart from these a new economic class, comprising four sectors, has been on the rise for more than a decade now. It consists of:

  • *The private sector:* MLW-Bombardier, the Banque Canadienne Nationale, the Provincial Bank, Trust Général du Canada.
  • *The co-operatives:* the Co-op-Fédérée, the Granby Co-op, the Mouvement Desjardins.
  • *The "mixed" sector:* Marine Industries.
  • *The state sector:* Sidbec, Hydro-Quebec.

These interests control a scant twenty per cent of the Quebec economy. Their principal frame of reference and power is the Quebec state. On the one hand these economic interests, like any good business, are looking for growth and immediate profits. The Liberal party took good care of them but by not offering any vision of the future, it condemned them to remain marginal. On the other hand, the Parti Québécois offered these ambitious social forces a kind of liberation. Now the PQ must try to convince these elements that its program best responds to their long-term aspirations. This program, with its emphasis on small and medium-sized business, the co-operative sector and, most important, on state-owned corporations, offers the only road to those who want to become "masters in their own house."

Ottawa's overtures to foreign countries and its attitude of independence from the U.S. may be understood as an attempt to conquer new markets in western Europe, Japan and Latin America. Sometimes this has even been done in open competition with the American multinationals. To ensure the consolidation of these large enterprises it is necessary, on the other hand, to go beyond the very concept of federalism, a concept that for some people is obsolete, to arrive at a kind of "jacobinism," or all-out centralism. This is the background to the real stakes of the November 15 election.

Postscript

On May 10, 1976, Prime Minister Trudeau confidently told a group of foreign visitors to Canada: "The separatist party in Quebec is now saying: if you elect us, we will hold a referendum to see if people want to separate. Well, to me, that is the end of separatism." Six months later, on November 15, the people around Trudeau were saying distractedly: "It isn't the end . . . it isn't over yet."

Trudeau must have been examining his conscience that night, thinking back to the role he had played in the downfall of his friend Bourassa. He reassured himself by saying that the people of Quebec had voted against an unpopular provincial administration. Were the voters thinking the same thing? Did they hold Bourassa responsible for unemployment, inflation, and Ottawa's refusal to pay its share of the Olympic deficit, not to mention the failure of bilingualism in the skies of Quebec?

Was Trudeau so short-sighted that he didn't see the rise of the new social forces behind the PQ's coming to power? How does he explain the breakdown of the Liberal machine that in the past had been so effective? Since Trudeau doesn't answer questions of this kind we are obliged to do so in his place.

We must also remember that he would be making a grave miscalculation if he estimates the strength of the PQ in any referendum at less than forty per cent of the popular vote. It should be noted that the PQ has made constant progress in popular favour since 1970, even with its clearly pro-independence platform. It went from twenty-three per cent of the vote in the 1970 election to thirty per cent in 1973 — when the question of a referendum on independence hadn't even been raised yet. Even if the idea of independence seems to have been watered down for the 1976 election, with the provision for the referendum, it's hard to imagine that independence forces haven't been making progress over the past three years, three years when Canadian federalism hasn't seemed to provide many advantages for most people in Quebec.

Obviously the international economic situation played an important role in the deterioration of the situation, but still the voters must assign a large part of the blame to Ottawa. In this same three-year period there has been confirmation that Canadian bilingualism is possible only in Quebec. For the other provinces, it's utopian to think about it. Quebecers have had the distinct impression that they are the only ones who practise the noble principles of bilingualism and federalism. The contemptuous attitude of people such as the members of CALPA and CATCA have only reinforced this feeling.

In addition, the Lévesque government will probably be one of the best provincial governments Canada has ever had. It is highly likely that the new Premier will show more concern for the people than Bourassa and his predecessors did. The PQ will do everything it can to make people happy, and may well succeed in large measure. When the referendum comes along this will be important in determining how people vote. In such a context it shouldn't be surprising if the question of confidence in the government is the key element in the referendum.

As we have seen, there's lots for Ottawa and English Canada to do in the next three or four years if they want to keep Quebec within Confederation. There is now an independentist government in one of the Canadian provinces, and it possesses the means to put on trial the kind of federalism practised by Trudeau since 1968. It will be a trial that risks turning to the disadvantage of Canada.

A hundred and twenty-five miles away from Montreal — in Ottawa — people seem unable to grasp the day-to-day reality of Quebec. That, and not the outcome of the November 1976 election which the prime minister referred to as a "return to tribalism," is the real tragedy in Canadian politics.

APPENDIX 1

For an Independent Quebec
by Réné Lévesque

reprinted from **Foreign Affairs,** *July 1976*

What does Quebec want? The question is an old cliché in Canadian political folklore. Again and again, during the more than 30 years since the end of World War II, it's been raised whenever Quebec's attitudes made it the odd man out in the permanent pull and tug of our federal-provincial relations. In fact, it's a question which could go back to the British conquest of an obscure French colony some 15 years before American Independence, and then run right through the stubborn survival of those 70,000 settlers and their descendants during the following two centuries.

By now, there are some six million of them in Canada, not counting the progeny of the many thousands who were forced by poverty, especially around the turn of the century, to migrate to the United States, and now constitute substantial "Franco" communities in practically all the New England states.

But Quebec remains the homeland. All along the valley of the St. Lawrence, from the Ottawa River down to the Gaspé peninsula and the great Gulf, in the ancient settlements which grew into the big cities of Montreal and Quebec, in hundreds of smaller towns and villages from the American border to the mining centres and power projects in the north, there are now some 4.8 million "Québécois." That's 81 per cent of the population of the largest and second most populous of Canada's ten provinces.

What does this French Quebec want? Sometime during the next few years, the question may be answered. And there are growing possibilities that the answer could very well be — independence.

Launched in 1967-68, the Parti Québécois, whose platform is based on political sovereignty, now fills the role of Her Majesty's loyal Opposition in the National Assembly — as we nostalgically designate our provincial legislature. In its first electoral test in 1970, it already had had 24 per cent of the votes. Then in 1973, a second general election saw it jump to 30 per cent, and, although getting only six out of 110 seats, become what our British-type parliamentary system calls the Official Opposition, i.e., the government's main interlocutor and challenger.

The next election might come any time now; this year in the fall, just after the Montreal Olympics, or at the latest in the fall of 1977. Whenever it does, all available indicators, including an impressive series of public opinion polls, tell us that for the first time the outcome is totally uncertain. The present provincial government, a branch of that same Liberal Party which also holds power at the federal level under Pierre Elliott Trudeau, is obviously on the way out. It has been in power for six years, and ever since its second and Pyrrhic victory in 1973 (102 seats) it has been going steadily downhill. Apart from a host of social and economic troubles, some imported but many more of its own making, there is around it a pervasive smell of incompetence and corruption. The scandal-ridden atmosphere surrounding the Olympic construction sites, and the incredible billion-dollar deficit which is now forecast, are just the most visible aspects of a rather complete political and administrative disaster.

Looking for an alternative, the French voter is now leaning quite clearly toward the Parti Québécois. In that "national" majority, we are at least evenly matched with Premier Robert Bourassa's Liberals, and probably ahead. As for the Anglophone minority of over a million people, whose natural attachment to the status quo normally makes them the staunchest supporters of the reigning federalist party, they are confused as never before. Composed of a dwindling proportion of Anglo-Saxon descendants of eighteenth-century conquerors or American Loyalists, along with those of nineteenth-century Irish immigrants, and a steadily growing "ethnic" mosaic (Jewish, Italian, Greek, etc.), in the crunch most of this minority will probably end up, as usual, supporting the Liberals. But not with the traditional unanimity. Caught between the Charybdis of dissatisfaction and the Scylla of secessionism, many are looking for some kind of "third force." Others, especially among younger people, are ready to go along with the Parti Québécois, whose minority vote should be a little less marginal next time than last.

So, all in all, there is quite a serious possibility that an "independentist" government will soon be elected in Quebec. At first sight, this looks like a dramatically rapid development, this burgeoning and flowering over a very few years of a political emanicipation movement in a population which, until recently, was commonly referred to as quiet old Quebec. But in fact, its success would mean, very simply, the normal healthy end result of a long and laborious national evolution.

II

There was the definite outline of a nation in that small French colony which was taken over, in 1763, by the British Empire at its apogee. For over a century and a half, beginning just before the Pilgrim Fathers landed in the Boston area, that curious mixture of peasants and adventurers had been writing a proud history all over the continent. From Hudson Bay to the Gulf of Mexico, and from Labrador to the Rockies, they had been the discoverers, the fur-traders, the fort-builders. Out of this far-ranging saga, historically brief though it was, and the tenacious roots which at the same time were being sunk into the St. Lawrence lowlands, there slowly developed an identity quite different from the original stock as well as from France of the *ancien régime;* just as different, in its way, as the American identity had become from its own British seeds. Thus, when the traumatic shock of the conquest happened, it had enough staying power to survive, tightly knit around its Catholic clergy and its country landowners.

Throughout the next hundred years, while English Canada was being built, slowly but surely, out of the leftovers of the American Revolution and as a rampart against America's recurrent attacks of Manifest Destiny, French Quebec managed to hang on — mostly because of its "revenge of the cradles." It was desperately poor, cut off from the decision-making centers both at home and in Great Britain, and deprived of any cultural nourishment from its former mother country. But its rural, frugal society remained incredibly prolific. So it grew impressively, at least in numbers. And it held on obstinately, according to its lights and as much as its humble means made it possible, to those two major ingredients of national identity — land and language. The hold on land was at best tenuous and, as in any colonial context, confined to the multitude of small farm holdings. Everything else — from the growth of major cities to the setting-up of manufacturing industries and then the rush of resource development — was the exclusive and undisputed field of action of "les

Anglais,'' the growing minority of Anglo-Saxon and then assimilated immigrant groups who ran most of Quebec under the compact leadership of Montreal-based entrepreneurs, financiers and merchant kings.

As for the French elite, it remained mostly made up of doctors, lawyers, and priests — ''essential services'' for the bodies and souls of cheap labor, whose miraculous birthrate kept the supply continuously overabundant. And naturally, there were politicians, practically all of that typical colonial breed which is tolerated as long as it keeps natives happily excited about accessories and divided on essentials.

Needless to say, the educational system was made both to reflect this type of society and to keep it going nicely and quietly. There was a modest collection of church-run seminaries, where the main accent was on recruiting for the priesthood, and which, for over a century, led to just one underdeveloped university. For nine-tenths of the children, there was nothing but grammar school, if that. Read and write barely enough to sign your name, and then, without any time for ''getting ideas,'' graduate to obedient respectful employment by any boss generous enough to offer a steady modest job.

Such was the culturally starved and economically inferior, but well-insulated and thus highly resistant, French Quebec which, 109 years ago, was led into the final mutation of British North America and its supreme defense against American expansionism: Confederation, of four eastern colonies as a beginning, but soon to run north of the border ''from sea to sea.'' Into that impressive Dominion, originally as one of four and eventually one of ten provinces, Quebec was incorporated without trouble and generally without enthusiasm. From now on, it was to be a minority forever, and, with the help of a dynamic federal immigration policy, a steadily diminishing one. In due time, it would probably merge and disappear into the mainstream, or at the most remain as a relatively insignificant and yet convenient ghetto: *la différence*.

As the building of Canada accelerated during the late nineteenth and early twentieth centuries, a tradition was established that Quebec was to get its measured share of the work, anytime there was enough to go around — and the same for rewards. And so, in a nutshell, it went until fairly recently. All told, it hasn't been such a bad deal, this status of "inner colony" in a country owned and managed by another national entity. Undoubtedly, French Quebec was (as it remains to this day) the least ill-treated of all colonies in the world. Under a highly centralized federal system, which is much closer to a unitary regime than American federalism, it was allowed its full panoply of provincial institutions: cabinet, legislature, courts, along with the quasi-permanent fun of great squabbles, usually leading to exciting election campaigns, about the defense or extension of its "state rights"! On three occasions during the last 80 years, one of "its own" has even been called upon — at times when there was felt a particular need to keep the natives quiet — to fill the most flattering of all offices, that of federal Prime Minister. Last but not least of the three, Mr. Trudeau, of whose "Canadian nationalism" it is naturally part and parcel, did as splendidly as was humanly possible for most of the last ten years in this big-chief-of-Quebec dimension of the job. But the law of diminishing returns, along with the inevitable way of all (including political) flesh, has been catching up with his so-called French Power in Ottawa. And no replacement seems to be in sight.

III

But this is getting ahead of our story. To understand the rise of Quebec's own new nationalism and its unprecedented drive toward self-government, we must go back to at least as far as World War II. Not that the dream had completely vanished during the two long centuries of survival which have just been described — from an admittedly partisan, but, I honestly believe, not unfair viewpoint. In the 1830s, for instance, there even was an ill-advised and disastrous armed rebellion by a few hundred "Patriots," leading to bloody repression and lasting memories about what not to do. And it is rather significant, by the way, that it took until just now before the poor heroic victims of that abortive rebellion became truly rehabilitated in popular opinion.

Small and impotent though it was, and in spite of feeling that this condition would possibly last forever, French Quebec never quite forgot the potential nation it had once been, never quite gave up dreaming about some miracle which might bring back its chance in the future. In some distant, indescribable future. Now and then, there were stirrings: a writer here, a small political coterie there; a great upsurge of nationalist emotions, in the 1880s, around the Riel affair — the hanging by "les Anglais" of the French-speaking leader of the Prairie Metis; then in 1917, on the conscription issue, a bitter and frequently violent confrontation between the Empire-minded English and the "isolationist" French; faint stirrings again in the Twenties; stronger ones in the Thirties.

Then World War II, with a repeat, in 1944, of the total disagreement on conscription. But mostly, here as elsewhere, this most terrible of all wars was also a midwife for revolutionary change. Thankfully in less disruptive a manner than in other parts of the world, it did start a revolution in Quebec. Wartime service, both overseas and on the industrial home-front, dealt a mortal blow to the old order, gave an irresistible impetus to urbanization and started the breakup of the traditional rural-parish ideal, yanked women by the thousands into war-plant industry and as many men into battle-dress discovery of the great wide world. For a small cooped-up society, this was a more traumatic experience than for most others. And then when the post war years brought the Roaring Fifties, unprecedented mobility, and television along with a consumer society, the revolution had to become permanent.

The beginning of the 1960s saw it baptized officially: the Quiet Revolution, with the adjective implying that "quaint old Quebec" couldn't have changed all that much. But it had. Its old set of values literally shattered, it was feeling collectively naked, like a lobster during its shedding season, looking frantically about for a new armour with which to face the modern world. The first and most obvious move was toward education. After so prolonged and scandalous a neglect of this most basic instrument of development, it was quickly realized that here was the first urgent bootstrap operation that had to be launched. It was done with a vengeance: from one of the lowest in the Western world, Quebec per capita investment in education rapidly became, and remains, one of the very highest. Not always well spent (but who is to throw the first stone?), with many mistakes along the way, and the job still far from complete, which it will never be anyway; but the essential results are there, and multiplying: human resources that are, at long last, getting required development, along with a somewhat equal chance for all and a normal furious rise in general expectations. The same, naturally, is happening also in other fields, quite particularly in that of economics, the very first where such rising expectations were bound to strike against the wall of an entrenched colonial setup, with its now intolerable second-class status for the French majority, and the stifling remote control of nearly all major decisions either in Ottawa or in alien corporate offices.

Inevitably, there had to be a spillover into politics. More than half of our public revenue and most of the decisions that count were and are in outside hands, in a federal establishment which was basically instituted not by or for us, but by others and, always first and foremost, for their own purposes. With the highly centralized financial system that this establishment constitutionally lords over, this means, for example, that about 80 per cent of Quebec savings and potential investment capital ends up in banks and insurance companies whose operations are none of our business. It also means, just for example once again, that immigration is also practically none of our business; and this could have, and is having, murderous effects on a minority people with a birthrate, changed like everything else in less than a generation, down from its former prodigious level to close to zero population growth.

Throughout the 1960s, these and other problems were interminably argued about and batted back and forth between federal politicians and bureaucrats ("What we have we hold, until we get more") and a succession of insistent but orthodox, no more than rock-the-boat, nationalists in Quebec. But while this dialogue of the deaf was going on and on, the idea of political independence reappeared as it had to. Not as a dream this time, but as a project, and very quickly as a serious one. This developed by leaps and bounds from easily ridiculed marginal groups to small semi-organized political factions, and finally to a full-fledged national party in 1967-68. These were the same two years during which, by pure coincidence, Mr. Trudeau was just as rapidly being elevated to the heights as a new federalist champion from Quebec.

But in spite of his best efforts and those of his party's branch-plant in provincial government, and through an unceasing barrage of money, vilification and rather repugnant fear-inducing propaganda, the voters have democratically brought the Parti Québécois ever closer to power. Which brings us right back to our starting-point . . .

IV

Let us suppose it does happen, and Quebec peacefully elects such a government. What then?

The way we see it, it would have to go somewhat like this. There is a new Quebec government which is totally dedicated to political independence. But this same Quebec, for the time being, is still very much a component of federal Canada, with its quite legitimate body of elected representatives in Ottawa. This calls, first of all, for at least a try at negotiation. But fruitful talk between two equally legitimate and diametrically opposed levels of government, without any further pressure from the population — that would be a real first in Canadian political history! Obviously, there would have to be the referendum which the Parti Québécois proposes in order to get the decisive yes-or-no answer to the tired question: What *does* Quebec want? (This was precisely the procedure by which the only new province to join Confederation during our recent democratic past, Newfoundland, was consulted in 1948-49 about whether or not to opt in. So why not about opting out?) If the answer should be no, then there's nothing to do but wait for the momentum of change to keep on working until we all find out whether or not there is finally to be a nation here. If the answer is yes, out, then the pressure is on Ottawa, along with a rather dramatic surge of outside attention, and we all get a privileged opportunity to study the recently inked Helsinki Declaration and other noble documents about self-determination for all peoples.

Fully confident of the basic integrity of Canadian democracy, and just as conscious that any silliness would be very costly for both sides, we firmly believe that the matter would then be brought to a negotiated settlement. Especially since the Parti Québécois, far from aiming at any kind of mutual hostility or absurd Berlin Wall, will then repeat its standing offer of a new kind of association, as soon as it is agreed to get rid of our illusion of deep unshakeable national unity, when in fact here are two quite real and distinct entities in an obsolete and increasingly morbid majority/minority relationship. Our aim is simply full equality by the only means through which a smaller nation can reasonably expect to achieve it with a larger one: self-government. But we are definitely not unaware of the shock waves that such a break, after so long an illusion of eternity, is bound to send through the Canadian political fabric.

We do not accept the simplistic domino theory, where Quebec's departure is presented as the beginning of fatal dislocation, with "separatism" spreading in all directions like a galloping disease until the balkanized bits and pieces are swallowed up by the huge maw next door. In spite of the somewhat unsure character of its national identity and its excessive satellization by the American economic and cultural empire, Canada-without-Quebec has enough "différence" left, sufficient traditions and institutional originality, to withstand the extraction of its "foreign body" and find a way to go on from there. It might even turn out to be a heaven-sent opportunity to revamp the overcentralized and ridiculously bureaucratized federal system, that century-old sacred cow which, for the moment, nobody dares to touch seriously for fear of encouraging Quebec's subversive leanings!

Be that as it may, we know there would be a traumatic moment and a delicate transition during which things might go wrong between us for quite a while, or else, one would hope, start going right as never before. With this strange new-coloured Quebec on the map between Ontario and the Maritime provinces, Canada must be kept from feeling incurably "Pakistanized," so we must address ourselves without delay to the problem of keeping a land bridge open with as much free flow of people and goods as is humanly possible; as much and more as there is, I would imagine, between Alaska and the main body of the United States over the western land bridge.

Such a scenario would call, as a decisive first step, for a customs union, as full-fledged as both countries consider to be mutually advantageous. We have, in fact, been proposing that ever since the Parti Québécois was founded, and naturally meeting with the most resonant silence in all orthodox federalist circles. But in the midst of that silence, not a single responsible politician, nor for that matter a single important businessman, has been heard to declare that it wouldn't happen if and when the time comes. For indisputably such a partnership, carefully negotiated on the basis of equality, is bound to be in the cards. Nothing prevents one envisaging it, for instance, going immediately, or at least very quickly, as far as the kind of monetary union which the European Common Market, with its original six and now nine members, has been fitfully aiming at for so many years. And building on this foundation, it would lead this new "northern tier" to a future immeasurably richer and more stimulating than the 109-year-old bind in which two nations more often than not feel and act like Churchill's two scorpions in the same bottle.

V

What of Quebec's own national future, both internal and international, in this context of sovereignty-cum-interdependence?

The answers here, for reasons that are evident, have to be brief, even sketchy and essentially tentative. The perspective of nationhood, for people who haven't been there yet, is bound to be an uncertain horizon. The more so in a period of history like ours, when so much is changing so fast you get the feeling that maybe change itself is becoming the only law to be counted on. Who can pretend to know exactly what or where his country will be 25 or even just ten years from now?

One thing sure, is that Quebec will not end up, either soon or in any foreseeable future, as the anarchic caricature of a revolutionary banana republic which adverse propaganda has been having great sinister fun depicting in advance. Either-Ottawa-or is very simply inspired by prejudice, the origin of this nonsense mostly to be found in the tragic month of October 1970 and the great "crisis" which our political establishments, under the astutely calculating Mr. Trudeau, managed to make out of a couple of dozen young terrorists, whose ideology was a hopeless hodgepodge of anarcho-nationalism and kindergarten Marxism, which had no chance of having any kind of serious impact. What they *did* accomplish was two kidnappings and, most cynically welcome of all, one murder — highly unfortunate but then also particularly par for the course in the international climate at the time. What was not par at all, however, was the incredible abuse of power for which those events, relatively minor per se, were used as a pretext: the careful buildup of public hysteria, army trucks rolling in during the night, and then, for months on end, the application in Quebec, and solely in Quebec, of a federal War Measures Act for which no peacetime precedent exists in any democratic country. A great spectacle produced in order to terrorize the Québécois forever back into unquestioning submissiveness, and, outside, to feed the mill of scary propaganda about how dangerous this tame animal could nevertheless be!

In actual fact, French Quebec, with its normal share of troubles, disquiet and, now, the same kind of social turmoil and search for new values that are rampant all over the Western world, remains at bottom a very solid, well-knit and nonviolent society. Even its new and demanding nationalism has about itself something less strident and essentially more self-confident than its current pan-Canadian counterpart. For Quebec has an assurance of identity, along with a relative lack of aggressiveness, which are the result of that one major factor of national durability lacking in the rest of Canada: a different language and the cultural fabric that goes with it.

Now how does the Parti Québécois see this society begin to find its way as an independent nation? What is the general outline of the political, social and economic structure we hope to bring forth? Serious observers have been calling our program basically social-democratic, rather comparable to the Scandinavian models although certainly not a carbon copy since all people, through their own experiencs, have to invent their own ''mix.''

The way we have been trying to rough it out democratically through half a dozen national party conventions, ours would call for a presidential regime, as much of an equal-opportunity social system as we could afford, and a decent measure, as quickly as possible but as carefully as indicated, of economic ''repatriation.'' This last would begin to happen immediately, and normally without any great perturbation, through the very fact of sovereignty: with the gathering in of all of our public revenues and the full legislative control which any self-respecting national state has to implement over its main financial institutions, banks, insurance companies and the like. In the latter case, this would allow us to break the stranglehold in which the old British-inspired banking system of just a handful of "majors" has always kept the people's money and financial initiative. The dominant position in our repatriated financial circuit would be handed over to Quebec's cooperative institutions, which happen to be particularly well developed in that very field, and, being strongly organized on a regional basis, would afford our population a decent chance for better-balanced, responsible, democratic development. And that, by the way, is just one fundamental aspect of the kind of evolution toward a new economic democracy, from the lowest rung in the marketplace up to board-room levels, which all advanced societies that are not already doing so had better start thinking about in the very near future.

As to non-resident enterprise, apart from the universal minimums concerning incorporations and due respect for Quebec taxes, language and other classic national requirements, what we have been fashioning over the last few years is an outline of a policy which we think is both logical and promising. It would take the form of an "investment code," giving a clean-cut picture, by sectors, of what parts of our economic life (e.g., culturally oriented activities, basic steel and forest resources) we would insist on keeping under home ownership, what other parts we would like to see under mixed control (a very few selected but strategic cases) and, finally, the multitude of fields (tied to markets, and to technological and/or capital necessities) where foreign interests would be allowed to stay or to enter provided they do not tend to own us along with their businesses.

In brief, Quebec's most privileged links, aside from its most essential relationship with the Canadian partner, would be first with the United Sates — where there is no imaginable reason to frown on such a tardy but natural and healthy development (especially during a Bicentennial year). Then Quebec would look to other Francophone or "Latin" countries as cultural respondents, and to France herself — who would certainly not be indifferent to the fact that this new nation would constitute the second most important French-speaking country in the world. In brief, such is the peaceful and, we confidently hope, fruitfully progressive state which may very well appear on the map of North America before the end of the decade.

APPENDIX 2

Portrait of the PQ Cabinet

René Lévesque, the new Premier of Quebec, introduced his cabinet in the Red Chamber of the National Assembly on Friday, November 26, 1976. Here is a brief sketch of the careers of each of them, along with those of a few other people who will play a role in the political life of Quebec in the next few years.

RENE LEVESQUE, Premier. Born August 24, 1922 in New Carlisle in the Gaspé. Studied law at Laval University (did not graduate). Served as correspondent attached to the American Armed Forces in London during World War II. Was one of the first journalists to enter the concentration camp at Dachau. In Milan, he was one of those to witness the anger of the crowd gathered around the hanged body of Mussolini. When he returned to Canada he worked for the CBC International Service (1946-1951), and in 1952 covered the Korean War. Between 1956 and 1959 he became well known as host of a widely followed TV program, *Point de Mire,* on Radio-Canada. The Radio-Canada producers' strike in 1958-59 showed him to be an accomplished leader. He was ready for politics. In 1960 he ran in the Montreal riding of Laurier for the Liberals. After the surprise

Liberal victory, Premier Jean Lesage invited him to join the cabinet and assigned him the new department of Natural Resources. In this portfolio he carried out the prickly task of nationalizing electricity in Quebec. In 1965 he was transferred to the department of the Family and Social Welfare, where he stayed until the defeat of his party in 1966. Throughout those years he played a front-line role in the Quiet Revolution. He left the Liberal party in 1967 — the same year that the late General de Gaulle uttered his "liberating" cry of "Vive le Québec libre!" — to found the Mouvement Souveraineté-Association. His profession of faith on the subject of the future of Quebec can be found in his best-seller published that same year, *An Option for Quebec*. In 1968 he brought together the scattered forces favouring independence as the Parti Québécois. He remained leader of the party although he twice failed to be elected to a seat in the Assembly, running in the ridings of Laurier in 1970 and Dorion in 1973.

JACQUES-YVON MORIN, Vice-Premier and Minister of Education. Born July 15, 1931. Did graduate studies at the University of Montreal, McGill, Harvard and Cambridge. Admitted to the Bar in 1952. A major interest has been teaching international and constitutional law. From 1964 to 1968 he was a member of the International Court of Arbitration at the Hague. From 1966 to 1969 he was president of the Estates-General of French Canada. In 1969 he directed the Institut Européen des Hautes Études Internationales at Nice. President of the Mouvement National des Québécois in 1972. Elected MNA for Sauvé in 1973, and served as Leader of the Opposition in the National Assembly until 1976. A serene man, a humanist and a diplomat.

ROBERT BURNS, Parliamentary leader and Minister of State for Parliamentary Reform. Born September 5, 1936. A lawyer, specializing in labour relations. Technical advisor and subsequently director of legal services for the CNTU until his election as MNA for Maisonneuve in 1970.

CLAUDE MORIN, Minister of Intergovernmental Affairs. Born in 1929. Did advanced studies in economics at Laval University. MA from Columbia University. Professor at Laval and at l'Ecole Nationale d'Administration Publique (University of Quebec). Economic advisor to the Quebec cabinet from 1961 to 1963. Until 1967, deputy minister of Federal-Provincial Affairs, then of Intergovernmental Affairs, the new name given to this portfolio. He introduced the subject of the referendum at the PQ's national convention in 1974. A methodical, rather distant man, he will play a key role in constitutional negotiations with Ottawa.

JACQUES PARIZEAU, Minister of Finance and Minister of Revenue. Born in 1930. Did advanced studies at the Institut d'Études Politiques in Paris, got his doctorate in economics from the London School of Economics. Conducted research for the Bank of Canada and the Royal Commission on Banking and Finance. Acted in various advisory roles between 1961 and 1965 for the departments of Finance, Natural Resources and Education. Economic and financial advisor to the Cabinet from 1961 to 1967; advisor to the Office of the Premier. For several years, directed the Institut d'Économie Appliquée at the Ecole des Hautes Etudes Commerciales (HEC) in Montreal. Chairman of the Board of the defunct newspaper *Le Jour*. Member of the PQ from its beginning. Has sat on the executive. As Minister of Finance and Revenue he will be controlling the purse-strings.

CAMILLE LAURIN, Minister of State for Cultural Development. Born in 1922. Studied medicine at the University of

Montreal, specializing in psychiatry which he studied in Geneva, Boston and Paris. Reorganized the Department of Psychiatry at the University of Montreal. MNA for Bourget from 1970 to 1973.

PIERRE MAROIS, Minister of State for Social Development. Born in 1940. Studied law at the University of Montreal, then at l'Ecole Pratique des Hautes Etudes in Paris. Union representative on the CNTU. Worked with the Fédération des Associations Coopératives d'Économie Familiale until October 18, 1976.

BERNARD LANDRY, Minister of State for Economic Development. Born in 1937. Did advanced studies in law and economics at the University of Montreal and in Paris. Technical advisor to the Department of Natural Resources when René Lévesque was Minister. Member of the Ligue des Droits de l'Homme (equivalent of the Human Rights League). Lawyer for striking workers at Firestone and Canadian Gypsum.

JACQUES LEONARD, Minister of State for Planning. Born in 1936. Studied Commerce and Administration at Laval. Chartered Accountant. Taught at HEC and the National University of Rwanda in Africa. Since 1968 has occupied various positions, including that of Vice-Dean of Continuing Education at the University of Montreal.

MARC-ANDRE BEDARD, Minister of Justice. Born in 1935. Sudied law at Laval and Ottawa. Practised law in Chicoutimi from 1960 until he was first elected to the National Assembly. Member of the PQ since its foundation.

LUCIEN LESSARD, Minister of Transportation and Public Works. Born in 1938. Obtained degree in social sciences from Laval. MNA for Saguenay since 1970.

MARCEL LEGER, Minister responsible for the Environment. Born in 1930. Obtained diploma in administration from the University of Montreal. Career as administrator for various companies. MNA for Lafontaine since 1970. Besides looking after the PQ's financing he was responsible for electoral organization between 1972 and 1974.

CLAUDE CHARRON, Minister responsible for the High Commission on Youth, Recreation and Sports. Born in 1946. MNA for St-Jacques since 1970.

GUY JORON, Minister reponsible for Energy, including Hydro-Québec. Born in 1940. Obtained BA in political science from University of Montreal. Vice-president of a brokerage house. Member of the Montreal Stock Exchange. From 1965 to 1970, acted as investment advisor and financial analyst. MNA for Gouin from 1970 to 1973. Author of a mordant analysis of Quebec, *La Course à la Folie* (The Race to Madness). The only member of the cabinet to have had frequent, daily contacts with the business world.

LISE PAYETTE, Minister of Consumer Affairs, Co-operatives and Financial Institutions. Born in 1931. Well known host of TV programs, *Place aux femmes* and *Appelez-moi Lise*. Ardent supporter of worker-run knitting factory, Tricofil. Presided over the St. Jean Baptiste Day celebrations in 1975 — a resounding success.

JEAN GARON, Minister of Agriculture. Born in 1938. Obtained MA in social sciences and law degree from Laval. From 1970, taught fiscal law, economics and co-operative law at Laval. His political roots go back to the beginning of the Rassemblement pour l'Indépendance Nationale.

DENIS LAZURE, Minister of Social Affairs. Born in 1925. Specialist in psychiatry. Director-general of the Rivière-des-Prairies Hospital and head of the departments of psychiatry at Sainte-Justine and Louis-Hyppolite-Lafontaine hospitals. Member of special commissions on psychiatry for the World Health Organization. He has inherited a very complex department: he is expected to adopt a less technocratic style than his predecessor, Claude Forget.

GUY TARDIF, Minister of Municipal Affairs. Born in 1935. Did advanced studies in criminology at the University of Montreal. Professor of Criminology at U of M. Particularly interested in problems of penitentiaries and police forces. Author of a book that attracted considerable attention, *Police et Politique au Québec.* The PQ has promised an inquiry into the administration of the City of Montreal, and naming a criminologist to this post is a good omen.

JACQUES COUTURE, Minister of Labour and Manpower and Minister of Immigration. Born in 1929. Studied law, philosophy and theology at Laval and Montreal. Social animator in working-class Saint-Henri since 1963, a Jesuit who has worked as a delivery-man and manual labourer in a factory. Community organizer for social services in Saint-Henri from 1973 to 1975. Spent a year in Grenoble to further his knowledge of urban sciences. Ran for the mayoralty of Montreal of 1974 against Jean Drapeau, as candidate for the opposition Montreal Citizens' Movement. Picked up forty per cent of the popular vote. Reaction to his appointment at Minister of Labour was one of surprise. Very different from his predecessors, he was seen the morning after his appointment walking his dog along Saint-Ferdinand Street in Saint-Henri, as usual.

LOUIS O'NEILL, Minister of Cultural Affairs and Minister of Communications. Born in 1925. Studied philosophy and theology at Laval and in Rome. Taught at the Séminaire de Québec and at Laval. Has belonged to a number of organizations, including the Comité Québec-Vietnam. Spent two years at the National University of Rwanda as Professor. Contributed to the magazine *Maintenant*.

YVES BERUBE, Minister of Natural Resources and Minister of Lands and Forests. Born in 1940. Graduate of the Massachusetts Institute of Technology. Conducted research on pollution and mining problems. Will he be put in charge of nationalizing the asbestos industry?

RODRIGUE TREMBLAY, Minister of Industry and Commerce. Born in 1939. Studied economics at Laval, Montreal and Stanford, where he obtained a master's degree and a doctorate. Economic advisor to the United Nations in 1975. Worked as an advisor to various African countries from 1970 to 1974, attempting to establish conditions for monetary co-operation between France and these countries. Has worked for the Bank of Canada, the Department of Consumer and Corporate Affairs in Ottawa, the Economic Council in Canada and the Canadian International Development Agency. Professor and head of the department of economics at University of Montreal. Author of a number of books, the best know being *Indépendance et Marché Commun Québec-E.U.* (Independence and a Quebec-U.S.A. Common Market).

YVES DUHAIME, Minister of Tourism, Fish and Game. Born in 1939. Studied law at McGill. Runs a beef farm.

DENIS DE BELLEVAL, Minister of the Public Service and Vice-President of the Treasury Board. Studied at Laval and the

London School of Economics. From 1970 to 1974, director general of the Quebec Office of Planning and Development. From 1974 to 1976, assistant to the Deputy Minister of Transport. Assistant director of the Bureau d'Aménagement du Réseau Express de Montréal (BAREM), a provincial government body working on the development of a new high-speed transportation system for the Montreal region.

Clément Richard, speaker of the National Assembly, is a lawyer who has acted for Les Gens de l'Air. Jean-Guy Cardinal, Minister of Education under Daniel Johnson and Jean-Jacques Bertrand, is Deputy Speaker. Jérôme Proulx is party whip.

Lévesque also made some innovations when he put together his cabinet. According to this "fundamental change in the internal workings of the cabinet" there is, along with the conventional cabinet, in which each minister has a specific, day-to-day administrative responsibility, a second cabinet called the "committee on priorities," composed of five "senior" Ministers of State. They will not be directly concerned with these day-to-day questions, but rather will be charged with establishing the list of priorities for the government, and seeing to the preparation and carrying out of broad-scale reforms. The Ministers of State are Robert Burns, Camille Laurin, Pierre Marois, Bernard Landry and Jacques Léonard, while Claude Morin and Jacques Parizeau also serve on the committee on priorities. These men will be Premier Lévesque's political advisors.